NBA STREET V3

Prima Games
A Division of Random House, Inc.

3000 Lava Ridge Court
Roseville, CA 95661
(800) 733-3000
www.primagames.com

NBA STREET V3

PRIMA OFFICIAL GAME GUIDE

Joe Grant Bell

The Prima Games logo is a registered trademark of Random House, Inc., registered in the United States and other countries. Primagames.com is a registered trademark of Random House, Inc., registered in the United States. Prima Games is a division of Random House, Inc.

Rosters are accurate as of December 17th, 2004.

Product Manager: Jill Hinckley
Editor: Amanda Peckham
Layout & Design: Jody Seltzer, Bryan Neff

ISBN: 0-7615-5057-7
Library of Congress Catalog Card Number: 2004116619
Printed in the United States of America

05 06 07 08 GG 10 9 8 7 6 5 4 3 2 1

Acknowledgments

Thanks to the following people for their help in making this guide happen.

At EA:

Mike McCartney   Brian Hayes

Brandon Zien

At Prima:

Jill Hinckley   Amanda Peckham

Libby Larson   Jody Seltzer

Contents

INTRODUCTION

Street has returned to tempt your taste buds with its signature dish: high-flying streetball with a spicy dash of NBA talent, moves, and attitude. This time the recipe calls for more tricks, more dunks, more options, and deeper play. Hope you're hungry.

This guide is your ultimate reference to *NBA STREET V3*, leading you all the way from fundamentals to the sizzle of prime time. Check out chapters on controls, game types, and the Street Challenge; then graduate to chapters on advanced offense and defense, and check out the full rosters of NBA players and Legends. Finally, refer to the last chapter for a master list of unlockable swag.

NBA STREET V3 is a deceptive game: it's fun and freewheeling, but it's also got depth. Read on to master it. The playground is waiting...

MASTER THE CONTROLS

Before jumping into the fancy stuff, let's review the basics. You may know this stuff already (or *think* you know it), but check it out anyway. You might learn a few things here.

Master Controls List (All Systems)

Full-Time Controls

MOVE	PS2	XBOX	GAMECUBE
Move Player	D-Button or Left Analog Stick	Ⓛ	Ⓒ
Turbo	L2, L1, R2, R1	Ⓛ, Ⓡ, Click Ⓛ	L, R, Z
Grab Tip-Off	Any face button (ball at apex)	Any face button (ball at apex)	Any face button (ball at apex)
Dive for Loose Ball	Double-Tap Any Turbo	Double-Tap Any Turbo	Double-Tap Any Turbo
Pause Game	START	START	START

Offense

MOVE	PS2	XBOX	GAMECUBE
Shoot/Dunk/Layup	●	Ⓑ	Ⓑ
Pass	✕	Ⓐ	Ⓐ
Random Trick Move	■	Ⓧ	Ⓧ
Specific Trick Move	Any Combo of Turbos + Right Analog Stick in Any Direction	Any Combo of Turbos + Ⓡ in Any Direction	Any Combo of Turbos + C Stick in Any Direction

Offense (cont'd)

MOVE	PS2	XBOX	GAMECUBE
Gamebreaker	Two Turbos + ●	Two Turbos + Ⓑ	Two Turbos + Ⓑ
Call for Pick	R3	Click Ⓡ	← or →
Fake Shot	Tap ●	Tap Ⓑ	Tap Ⓑ
Off the Heezay	R1 + L1 + ✕	Ⓡ + Ⓛ + Ⓐ	R + L + Ⓐ
Off the Chest/Back	R1 + L2 + ✕	Ⓡ + Click Ⓛ + Ⓧ	R + Z + Ⓐ
Off The Footay/ Bootay	R2 + L2 + ✕	Ⓛ + Click Ⓛ + Ⓐ	L + Z + Ⓐ
Back to Papa	Any Two Turbos + ✕ Towards the Hoop	Any Two Turbos + Ⓐ Towards the Hoop	Any Two Turbos + Ⓐ Towards the Hoop
Special Kick Pass	L3 + ✕	Ⓛ + Ⓐ	Z + Ⓐ

Defense

MOVE	PS2	XBOX	GAMECUBE
Switch Players	✕	Ⓐ	Ⓐ
Block/Rebound*	▲	Ⓨ	Ⓨ
Turbo Block	▲ + Any Two Turbos	Ⓨ + Any Two Turbos	Ⓨ + Any Two Turbos
Steal	■ or Right Analog Stick in Any Direction except Up, Up-Left, Up-Right	Ⓧ or Ⓡ in Any Direction except Up, Up-Left, Up-Right	Ⓧ or C Stick in Any Direction except Up, Up-Left, Up-Right

*Note - Block/Rebound can also be performed by pressing the trick stick Up, Up-Left, or Up-Right

There are four turbo buttons on the PS2, and three on the other consoles. Hold down one or more turbo buttons while you're performing moves—for example, hold down turbo while dunking to turn a run-of-the-mill dunk into a monster throwdown.

Hold down more than one turbo at a time to perform more complicated moves. For example, press the trick stick by itself to perform a basic trick. Press the trick stick while holding a single turbo to do a fancier trick. Hold down two or more turbos while pressing the trick stick to pull off progressively fancier tricks.

The more turbos you hold down while performing a trick or dunk, the fancier—and harder—that trick or dunk is. You'll get more points for pulling off fancier moves—but fancier moves are also harder to pull off and use more turbo.

The turbo bar at the top of the screen shows you how much juice you've got at any given time. If you completely drain it, the bar takes about five seconds to fully recharge.

If you try a move that requires more turbo than you've got, the move won't happen (or you'll get the no-turbo version).

Grab Tip-Off

Tap this button to control the tip-off at the game's start.

MOVE	PS2	XBOX	GAMECUBE
Grab Tip-Off	Any face button (ball at apex)	Any face button (ball at apex)	Any face button (ball at apex)

Defense (cont'd)

MOVE	PS2	XBOX	GAMECUBE
Trick Counter*	■ + Any Two Turbos or Right Analog Stick Tap + Any Two Turbos	✗ + Two Turbos or ® Tap + Any Two Turbos	⟲ + Two Turbos or C Stick Tap + Any Two Turbos
Call for Double Team	R3	Click ®	← or →

Note - The Trick Counter can only be performed if you press the trick stick Left, Right, Left-Down, Right-Down, or Down.

Full-Time Controls

These controls never change, regardless of whether you're on offense or defense.

Move Player

MOVE	PS2	XBOX	GAMECUBE
Move Player	D-Button or Left Analog Stick	Ⓛ	⊚

Use the analog stick to move your currently selected player. Pretty simple, huh? Press lightly to walk; press hard to jog. But how, you ask, do you flat-out *run*? For that, you need turbo. Read on…

Turbo

MOVE	PS2	XBOX	GAMECUBE
Turbo	L2, L1, R2, R1	Ⓛ, ®, Click Ⓛ	Ⓛ, Ⓡ, Ⓩ

Turbo is central to *NBA STREET V3*. We discuss it a lot later on because using your turbo is possibly the most important skill in the whole game! So consider this section a very basic introduction to turbo.

Dive for Loose Ball

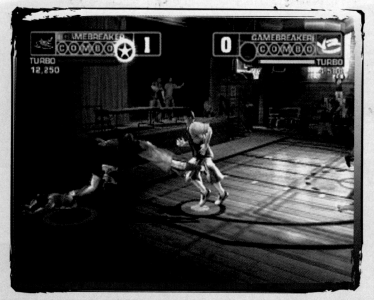

Double tap any turbo button to dive. This is *the* way to grab a loose ball, as it gets you to the ball faster than running.

MOVE	PS2	XBOX	GAMECUBE
Dive for Loose Ball	Double-Tap Any Turbo	Double-Tap Any Turbo	Double-Tap Any Turbo

NOTE

If the ball is a long way away, you might have to dive twice to get there.

Dive early and often, because the ball comes loose all the time. Steal attempts usually don't give you the ball outright; very often, the ball just gets poked loose. Then you must dive after it and take possession.

A player that screws up a trick usually coughs up the ball, too. That's another chance for you to show off your diving skills.

Pause Game and View Menu

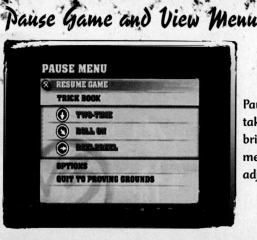

Pause the game to take a break, or to bring up the options menu and make adjustments.

MOVE	PS2	XBOX	GAMECUBE
Pause Game	START	START	START

Offense

NBA STREET V3 is all about spectacular offense: outlandish tricks, high-flying dunks, masterful trick passes, and deadly outside shooting. This section lays down the basics, starting with the moves you'll use all the time, and then moving down to more specialized stuff.

Shoot/Dunk/Layup

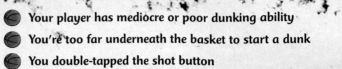

- Your player has mediocre or poor dunking ability

- You're too far underneath the basket to start a dunk

- You double-tapped the shot button

This button makes your player shoot, dunk, or layup. The exact move depends on where you are, what player you're controlling, and how many turbos you're holding down.

MOVE	PS2	XBOX	GAMECUBE
Shoot/Dunk/Layup	●	Ⓑ	Ⓑ

You shoot the ball (instead of dunking) if:

- You're too far from the basket to dunk

- You're close to the basket, but not moving toward it

- A defender is blocking your path to the basket

- You're *under* the basket or behind the backboard

TIP! *Your player's Shooting rating affects the chances of making a basket, but your timing makes a difference too. Release the shot button as your player approaches the top of his jump to increase the odds of a successful basket. We discuss other factors affecting shot accuracy in the Advanced Offense chapter.*

If you want to dunk instead of shoot the ball (and you usually do!), do the following:

- Be close enough to dunk (not out by the three-point line)

- Be jogging or running toward the basket

- Have a clear path to the basket (nobody in your way)

- Use turbos for a fancier dunk

High Dunking skill lets you do the fancier, multi-turbo dunks without screwing up. A player attempting a dunk beyond his capabilities almost always botches the dunk and turns the ball over.

Sometimes you think you've fulfilled all the conditions for a dunk, but your player performs a layup instead of dunking. Here are the situations where a player lays up instead of dunking:

That last one is important to remember: Tap the trick stick or tap the shot button a second time to convert a dunk into a layup. Usually you want to dunk and score trick points, but if you're about to get blocked, switching to a layup often lets you avoid the block.

TIP! *Always switch to a layup if your dunk is about to be blocked. It takes time to get used to this move, but it's worthwhile to practice. Remember: getting rejected not only prevents you from scoring, but it also gives the other team trick points!*

Pass

Pass frequently to find holes in the defense. If you constantly pass from one side of the basket to the other, you're more likely to get an open shot or easy drive to the lane.

If a teammate flies up to ridiculous heights, immediately press the pass button. You'll feed him for an alley-oop.

MOVE	PS2	XBOX	GAMECUBE
Pass	✕	Ⓐ	Ⓐ

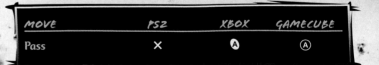

TIP: Alley-oops are easy, and they score lots of trick points. The trick is training yourself to pass in time; if you're caught up in some fancy maneuver, it's easy to miss your teammate skying for the oop. If you miss your chance, just let it go; passing too late usually results in a turnover.

Trick Moves

Trick moves are just what they sound like: funky streetball maneuvers that demonstrate your prowess with the rock. Trick moves serve two functions: they fake out the defender (if you're close enough to him when you perform the trick), and they get you trick points. Trick moves also help build up your GB meter. String a bunch of trick moves together, then finish it all off with a sweet shot or a fancy dunk to really rack up the trick points.

MOVE	PS2	XBOX	GAMECUBE
Random Trick Move	■	⊗	Ⓧ
Specific Trick Move	Any Combo of Turbos + Right Analog Stick in Any Direction	Any Combo of Turbos + right thumbstick in Any Direction	Any Combo of Turbos + C Stick in Any Direction

If your trick is successful, your defender might fall down, get pushed back, or get left behind. Or none of that might happen. But if you perform the move successfully, you'll always be awarded trick points.

There are tons of trick moves. They all look different and have different names, but don't get overwhelmed. The only thing that really matters is the number of turbos you press. No turbos gets you a basic trick, one turbo results in a fancier trick, and so on.

> **NOTE:** Every trick move is listed in the Advanced Offense chapter.

High Dunking skill lets you do the fancier, multi-turbo dunks without screwing up. A player attempting a dunk beyond his capabilities almost always botches the dunk and turns the ball over.

Sometimes you think you've fulfilled all the conditions for a dunk, but your player performs a layup instead of dunking. Here are the situations where a player lays up instead of dunking:

- Your player has mediocre or poor dunking ability
- You're too far underneath the basket to start a dunk
- You double-tapped the shot button

That last one is important to remember: Tap the trick stick or tap the shot button a second time to convert a dunk into a layup. Usually you want to dunk and score trick points, but if you're about to get blocked, switching to a layup often lets you avoid the block.

TIP: Always switch to a layup if your dunk is about to be blocked. It takes time to get used to this move, but it's worthwhile to practice. Remember: getting rejected not only prevents you from scoring, but it also gives the other team trick points!

Pass

Pass frequently to find holes in the defense. If you constantly pass from one side of the basket to the other, you're more likely to get an open
shot or easy drive to the lane.

If a teammate flies up to ridiculous heights, immediately press the pass button. You'll feed him for an alley-oop.

MOVE	PS2	XBOX	GAMECUBE
Pass	✕	Ⓐ	Ⓐ

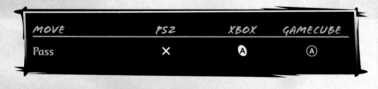

Alley-oops are easy, and they score lots of trick points. The trick is training yourself to pass in time; if you're caught up in some fancy maneuver, it's easy to miss your teammate skying for the oop. If you miss your chance, just let it go; passing too late usually results in a turnover.

Trick Moves

Trick moves are just what they sound like: funky streetball maneuvers that demonstrate your prowess with the rock. Trick moves serve two functions: they fake out the defender (if you're close enough to him when you perform the trick), and they get you trick points. Trick moves also help build up your GB meter. String a bunch of trick moves together, then finish it all off with a sweet shot or a fancy dunk to really rack up the trick points.

MOVE	PS2	XBOX	GAMECUBE
Random Trick Move	■	ⓧ	Ⓨ
Specific Trick Move	Any Combo of Turbos + Right Analog Stick in Any Direction	Any Combo of Turbos + right thumbstick in Any Direction	Any Combo of Turbos + C Stick in Any Direction

If your trick is successful, your defender might fall down, get pushed back, or get left behind. Or none of that might happen. But if you perform the move successfully, you'll always be awarded trick points.

There are tons of trick moves. They all look different and have different names, but don't get overwhelmed. The only thing that really matters is the number of turbos you press. No turbos gets you a basic trick, one turbo results in a fancier trick, and so on.

Every trick move is listed in the Advanced Offense chapter.

There are two ways to perform tricks. One is to press the trick button. The other is to push the trick stick in any direction (again, with or without turbos). The trick stick gives you finer control, because pushing the stick in a particular direction with a particular number of turbos allows you to *pick which trick you're going to do*. If you use the button instead of the stick, you just perform a *random* trick. Get in the habit of using the stick.

Gamebreaker

When your Gamebreaker meter fills up, it's hard not to notice. Not only does the meter start to flash, but the sky darkens. At this point, you may attempt a Gamebreaker.

MOVE	PS2	XBOX	GAMECUBE
Gamebreaker	Two Turbos + ●	Two Turbos + Ⓑ	Two Turbos + Ⓑ

Gamebreakers are shots or dunks that give you extra points and take away points from the opponent. The exact point swing depends on how tricky the Gamebreaker is; see the Advanced Offense chapter for details.

Each time you do a Gamebreaker, you need more trick points to trigger the next one. So it's hard to get a bunch of Gamebreakers in a single game.

Call for Pick

This button orders your AI-controlled teammates to set picks for you, hopefully allowing you to shake your defender. If the pick works, your defender will be pushed to the ground, leaving you wide-open for a shot or drive to the lane.

MOVE	PS2	XBOX	GAMECUBE
Call for Pick	R3	Click Ⓡ	← or →

Fake Shot

Tap the shot button (don't hold it!) to fake a shot. You can do this several times in a row, if you want to.

If your defender bites on your fake and jumps, shoot over him while he's coming down. If he doesn't buy it, you should probably pass. Otherwise, you're setting yourself up to get the ball stolen.

MOVE	PS2	XBOX	GAMECUBE
Fake Shot	Tap ●	Tap Ⓑ	Tap Ⓑ

Trick Passes

These trick passes allow you to rack up the trick points. Off the Heezay bounces the ball off your opponent's head, Off the Footay/Bootay bounces the ball off different body parts based on

whether your opponent is facing you or turned around, and Back to Papa bounces the ball off the backboard and back into your hands.

All these moves produce lots of trick points and set up powerful combos. But be careful about overusing them, especially against the AI opponent, which is great at using trick counters to break them up.

MOVE	PS2	XBOX	GAMECUBE
Off the Heezay	R1+L1+X	®+L+Ⓐ	R+L+Ⓐ
Off the Chest/Back	R1+L2+X	® + Click L + Ⓐ	R+Z+Ⓐ
Off the Footay/Bootay	R2+L2+X	L + Click L + Ⓐ	L+Z+Ⓐ
Back to Papa	Any Two Turbos + X Towards the Hoop	Any Two Turbos + Ⓐ Towards the Hoop	Any Two Turbos + Ⓐ Towards the Hoop

🏀 MASTER THE GAME 🏀

If a teammate is jumping for the alley-oop, quickly perform an Off The Heezay pass to bounce the ball off your opponent's head and up to the jumping teammate!

Defense

Offense is supposed to be fun; defense is supposed to be hard work. In reality, defense is a lot of fun too—especially if you like to frustrate your opponent.

NBA STREET V3 is geared toward offense, just like the real NBA. Don't expect to completely shut the other guys down, even if you're a good defensive player. Instead, try to prevent wide-open shots, limit your opponent's tricks and fancy dunks, and generate the occasional turnover. If you can do that, you're well on your way to victory.

Switch Players

MOVE	PS2	XBOX	GAMECUBE
Switch Players	X	Ⓐ	Ⓐ

Press this button to take control of a different player.

Why switch players? One good reason is to get into the action. Take control of the defensive player nearest the ball, so you can try to steal or defend a talented human player.

Another reason to switch: you don't have the right player for the job. Maybe you like to hang around the basket and swat away shots. You can't do that with a speedy ball handler, so switch to your monstrous center. Or maybe you've got a big guy but you want to challenge the opposing guard out by the three-point line. In that case you'd better switch to a player with good speed and handles, because the guard will blow right by your behemoth.

Block/Rebound

This button makes your player jump. If you're in position to block a shot, you'll do it. If you're in position to grab a rebound, you'll do that too. Just remember that this button gets your player vertical.

MOVE	PS2	XBOX	GAMECUBE
Block/Rebound*	▲	Ⓨ	Ⓨ

You won't automatically block every shot or rebound every ball, even if you're in the right position; your player's Block and Rebound stats have something to do with that. Still, you can maximize your chances by standing in the right place and timing your jump properly.

There is no goaltending violation in *NBA STREET V3*, so you can park right in front of the basket and block shots on their way down.

Turbo Block

Hold down two turbos while blocking, and you snatch the ball out of the air instead of swatting it away. This is great because you're guaranteed to get the turnover (with a regular block, the opponent can sometimes recover the ball).

MOVE	PS2	XBOX	GAMECUBE
Turbo Block	▲ + Any Two Turbos	Ⓨ + Any Two Turbos	Ⓨ + Any Two Turbos

You should turbo block whenever possible. Try to have a little turbo available at all times, so you can turbo block instead of doing a regular block.

Steal

Tap the steal button to swipe at the ball. Factors that affect your chance of success:

🏀 Your Steal skill
🏀 The opponent's Handles skill
🏀 Being close enough to the opponent
🏀 The position of the ball

MOVE	PS2	XBOX	GAMECUBE
Steal	■ or Right Analog Stick in Any Direction except Up, Up-Left, Up-Right	Ⓧ or Ⓐ in Any Direction except Up, Up-Left, Up-Right	Ⓧ or C Stick in Any Direction except Up, Up-Left, Up-Right

You're most likely to steal the ball if you tap the button when the ball is waist high—*not* while it's on the ground.

> *Steal attempts use up turbo—even if you fail, and even though it doesn't require you to press a turbo button. So don't swipe like a madman; pick your spots instead.*

A successful steal doesn't necessarily deliver the ball into your hands. Rather, you're likely to poke the ball out. If that happens, you need to track it down. Remember to dive!

Trick Counter

Press the steal button (or trick stick) in conjunction with any two turbo buttons to perform a trick counter. If you're close to an opponent who's starting a trick, the trick counter can automatically cancel that trick and swipe the ball.

As you might imagine, the trick counter is a powerful weapon. Use it to keep the opponent honest, preventing him from rattling off trick move after trick move and racking up major trick points.

MOVE	PS2	XBOX	GAMECUBE
Trick Counter*	■ + Any Two Turbos or Right Analog Stick Tap + Any Two Turbos	✕ + Two Turbos or Ⓡ Tap + Any Two Turbos	✗ + Two Turbos or C Stick Tap + Any Two Turbos

*Note - The Trick Counter can only be performed if you press the trick stick Left, Right, Left-Down, Right-Down, or Down.

> *Your chances of countering a trick go down with time. If you counter right as the opponent starts his trick, you're very likely to steal the ball. If you counter when the opponent is well into the trick, it's a lot less likely to work.*

Call for Double Team

This button calls an AI-controlled teammate to double-team the ball handler. This can be particularly useful when an opposing big guy with low handles has the ball.

MOVE	PS2	XBOX	GAMECUBE
Call for Double Team	R3	Click Ⓡ	← or →

GAME MODES & OPTIONS

There's lots of stuff to do in this game and at first it might seem a little overwhelming. Don't worry: this is where we make sense of it all.

Game On

Game On is a quick-action mode. Pick the number of players, select two teams, and go head-to-head or versus the CPU.

Game On doesn't offer many options; it's all about getting you onto the court as quickly as possible. If you want to change the game rules or pick individual players from each team, you should try a Pick-up Game instead.

Play it Modes

The meat of the game is under the main menu's Play It option. Here are the game modes you'll find there.

Pick-up Game

Pick-up Game is a full-featured version of Game On. Here you can do everything you did in Game On, plus you can choose a playground or gym, pick the individual players you want to play (instead of just the team), and adjust the rules to your liking.

You can really go nuts with rules changes. Here are your options.

Normal

A normal game has the following defaults:

- Game to 21
- Nobody gets spotted any points
- 24-second shot clock
- Long range shots worth 2
- Short range shots worth 1
- Dunks worth 1

You can change all these defaults. In other words, you can:

- Play to more or less than 21 points
- Spot points to a weaker player, as a handicap to the better player
- Adjust the shot clock duration or shut it off completely
- Independently adjust the point values of long and short range shots and dunks

In a Trick Point Challenge, you should milk the shot clock for all it's worth, performing tricks and funky passes until your time is almost up. Then finish with a high-value dunk, to maximize your trick points.

Since Gamebreaker dunks provide tons of trick points, the winner of a Trick Point Challenge is usually the player who's quickest to trigger Gamebreakers.

By changing the defaults, you can change the emphasis (and strategy) of the game. For example, to make dunks supreme, make them worth three points apiece and make all other shots only count for one. Play around with these settings and you'll find all sorts of bizarre combinations.

> **NOTE**
>
> You can adjust the target number of trick points and alter the shot clock in a Trick Point Challenge. You can also spot trick points to a weaker player to balance out a potentially unfair game. But you can't adjust the value of shots and dunks because the game has no score!

Trick Point Challenge

In a Trick Point Challenge, no score is kept. Instead, the winner is the first team that scores the target number of trick points. You'll still want to put the ball in the basket, of course, but only to finish off combos and score trick points.

Dunks Only

A Dunks Only game is just what it sounds like: a game where shots are worthless, and only dunks score real, honest-to-goodness scoreboard points.

You can't give shots a point value in a Dunks Only game, though you can adjust everything else, including the point value of dunks.

TIP? *Select your players wisely in a Dunks Only game. You might want to ditch your small, can't-dunk point guard in favor of another front-line player who can slam it home. If you have players that cannot dunk at all, you must be extremely careful to get it out of their hands when it's time to score. Accidentally shooting the ball is as bad as turning it over.*

TIP? *NBA Scoring decreases the value of long range shots. Instead of being worth twice the value of a short range shot or dunk, as in a typical game, they're only worth 50 percent more. As a result, you should go for more dunks and fewer long range shots.*

No Gamebreakers

This is a normal game, except that Gamebreakers don't happen. You can still do tricks, and you still earn trick points, but your Gamebreaker meter will not fill up. The result is a game where tricks are mainly useful for shaking a defender, and trick passes (Off the Heezay, Back to Papa) are not very useful. You'll want to concentrate on straight-ahead scoring, unless the game is well in hand.

Every rule of this game can be altered, just like a normal game.

NBA Scoring

NBA Scoring fixes long range shot values at three points, and other shots and dunks at two points. These point values can't be changed, though everything else can be.

Old School Scoring

In an Old School game, all shots are worth one point. So you *really* shouldn't bother with long range shots; just take any shot that's open. And remember that despite the old-time rules, Gamebreakers are still in effect. So rack up those trick points, as usual.

You can't adjust shot or dunk values in an Old School game, but other settings can be altered.

Gamebreaker Wins

A Gamebreaker Wins game gives the victory to the first team to score a Gamebreaker. Score isn't kept; it's all about filling up your Gamebreaker meter and activating that Gamebreaker.

If your opponent fills his Gamebreaker meter first, your only hope is to stall by playing keep-away during your possession. Then try to steal the ball and play keep-away some more, until your opponent's Gamebreaker opportunity has passed.

Since the actual amount of trick points doesn't matter in these games, don't get fancy in midair and risk screwing up your Gamebreaker dunk. Keep it nice and easy and score the victory.

Back to Basics

Back to Basics games don't score trick points at all. You can adjust any setting, including the point values of dunks and shots, but you don't need to worry about scoring points or getting Gamebreakers.

How is this game different from a No Gamebreakers contest? In a No Gamebreakers game, trick points are awarded—they just don't result in Gamebreakers. So you can still get Street Point bonuses for accumulating trick points. In a Back to Basics game, on the other hand, trick points don't happen at all.

Street Challenge

The Street Challenge is the heart of the single-player game. In it, you create a custom home playground and a custom baller. Then you assemble a team around your custom baller and go on a whirlwind tour of playgrounds and

gyms, playing in special events and tournaments whenever they pop up, or playing pick-up ball whenever nothing else is happening. You gradually improve your baller, your court, and your team, and when the dust clears, you hopefully end up a playground legend.

The next chapter is devoted entirely to Street Challenge, so that's all we'll say about it here.

Dunk Contest

Dunk Contests pit two or more ballers against each other in a dunking extravaganza. Each dunk is judged on creativity and technical difficulty and the dunker with the most points at the end wins.

Dunk Contest dunks are essentially just Gamebreaker dunks, with a few extras thrown in for good measure. What are those extras? First, there are ways to pass the ball to yourself, and then catch it in midair as you start the dunk; this gives you extra points. Second, you can put props on the court and dunk over them, though you'll fail your dunk if you bump into them.

Once you're airborne, you do the exact same tricks in a Dunk Contest that you do in a Gamebreaker.

Don't do the same tricks over and over. Mix it up to score maximum points.

The rule of thumb in a Dunk Contest is "more stuff equals more points." The more complicated tricks you do, and the more extras you tack on (passes to yourself, props), the more points you score. Of course, you won't get many points at all for a failed dunk, so you have to strike a balance and not bite off more than you can chew.

> **NOTE**
> A score below 10 is pretty bad and is usually reserved for a failed dunk. Scores between 10 and 20 are usually given to dunks that were successful, but not very tricky. Successful dunks that involved lots of tricks are usually scored in the 20s.

The Advanced Offense Chapter gives a complete list of Dunk Contest tricks and special passes. Study those moves to become a master of the Dunk Contest.

Practice

Select a baller of your choice (from lists of custom ballers, NBA stars, or all-time greats) and hit the playground solo. Practice mode allows you to try tricks and dunks in isolation and really study your moves. You can practice wicked combos here or work on mastering the trickiest skills—like top-tier, off-the-backboard dunks.

Play Online

If you're playing on a PlayStation®2, set up your network and your EA Account. Then create an EA Sports Persona and you're ready to play online. If you are on an Xbox®, just sign in using your gamertag.

Your online options are as follows:

- *Play:* You have several options. Two users can earn World Points playing World Challenge Mode. You can also play tracked games in the NBA Challenge and try to enhance your ranking on the leaderboard. Exhibition Mode and Dunk Contest games may also be played, but strictly for fun (no rankings or points).

- *Create Baller:* This is just like creating a baller for offline play, but the baller you create here is stored on the EA server. You cannot use an offline baller for online play; you must create one here.

- *Customization:* This is just like Customization for offline play. Create or modify a home court or upgrade your baller.

- *Leaderboard:* See how you stack up against other online players.

- *News:* Check out news on server status, game tweaks, and other important updates.

- *Online Settings:* Customize your online experience.

We recommend that you play some pick-up games and Street Challenge offline before leaping online. That way you'll be familiar with all the online options and you won't get spanked too badly by the veteran players you're sure to run into.

Create Baller

Creating a baller is an important part of the Street Challenge. Check out the Building the Perfect Baller section in the next chapter for details.

basket, including the stanchions (the things holding up the hoops); and make changes to the background.

Have fun here! Customizing a court is almost a whole game in itself.

Customization

Customization lets you tweak your created courts and ballers with an astounding variety of looks and gear.

V3 Store

The V3 store lets you buy stuff for your baller, using Street Points. Want a hat? How about a skullcap? Baggy pants? Maybe an official NBA jersey? Or some skin art? It's all here. The variety is endless.

Court Creator

This is where you design custom courts. Custom courts are available for pick-up games; also, you need a custom "home court" for every Street Challenge.

A basic court is free. Choose the city where it's located, and, boom, it appears. You can even tweak a few settings (like the background) for free. But most upgrades and custom elements must be purchased with Street Points.

TIP! Aside from just looking cool, customizing your baller's look has an important game purpose. Make each baller look distinct from everyone else on the court, and you'll never have trouble figuring out where he is (or who you're controlling).

Edit Skills

Street Points can be spent to upgrade your baller's skills. This is where you do it.

You can really customize the heck out of your courts. Change aspects of the court itself, including its surface, color, and lines; adjust the logo at center court; change aspects of the

Skills get costlier at higher levels, and your baller's height and weight have an effect on cost as well. See Building the Perfect Baller (in the next chapter) for more details.

Barber Shop

The barber shop lets you get creative with your baller's 'do. It's all here. Flat top? Check. Cornrows? Check. Clean shaven? Check. Big, bushy afro? Check. We're ready for takeoff…

Shoe Creator

If the standard selection of kicks doesn't float your boat, you can design your own. Start out with a basic Rbk or Adidas design, then modify every conceivable aspect, from the body to the heel to the laces. Then put 'em on your baller and you're ready to roll.

Save Wardrobe

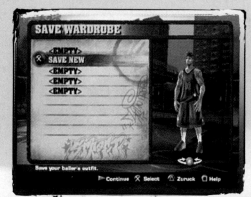

Changing every aspect of your baller's look takes time. Any time you have a particular outfit just the way you like it, save it to a wardrobe slot. Then you can change back and forth between your different looks effortlessly.

Create Team

Do you long to have Carmelo and LeBron on the same team? Do you dream of reuniting Vince Carter and Tracy McGrady? Fear not. Create a custom team using any current NBA players, custom ballers, and/or any Street Legends and NBA Legends you've unlocked. Then select that team for a pick-up game, and you're good to go.

Trick Book

Specific combinations of turbo buttons and the trick stick result in different tricks. The exact trick your baller performs depends on his trick book.

For example, let's say you're playing on the PS2. You simultaneously press two turbo buttons and push down on the trick stick. What trick gets performed? The default trick is All Good, so at first your baller does the trick called All Good.

Once your baller has successfully done an All Good in a game, that trick's Chapter Two version opens up. Go into the trick book and put a check mark next to the Chapter Two version, which is called Back to the Lab. Now, whenever you press two buttons and down on the trick stick, your baller does a Back to the Lab. So, whenever you successfully complete a trick in a combo, a trick in the next chapter is unlocked.

Once your baller has done a Back to the Lab in a combo in a game, the Chapter Three version of the trick opens up. Go into the trick book again and put a check mark next to the Chapter Three version, which is Street Wise. Now your baller will do a Street Wise.

The bottom line: once everything is unlocked, use the trick book to pick your favorite tricks, guaranteeing that those are the ones your baller will perform in games.

When you unlock Legends and courts, you make them available for pick-up games.

Unlocked Legends and courts have no effect on your current Street Challenge. For example, just because you unlocked Julius Erving doesn't mean you can throw him onto your Street Challenge team! And just because you unlocked a particular court doesn't mean you can now get there in a Street Challenge. To repeat, unlocked stuff is just for pick-up games.

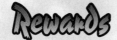

This is where you view rewards you've already collected, and unlock new ones. You can:

- Check high scores
- View and unlock NBA Legends
- View and unlock Street Legends
- View and unlock courts
- View earned dunk contest trophies

STREET CHALLENGE

Street Challenge is the heart of the single-player mode in this game. This is where you create a baller, assemble a team, and wage a full frontal assault on the nation's top playgrounds and streetball venues.

Overview of Street Challenge

Getting Started

Your first task in Street Challenge is to pick a team captain from your list of created ballers. If you haven't created a custom baller yet, you'll do so now.

Next, create or select a custom court. This serves as your "home court" during the Street Challenge.

Finally, pick two teammates from a pool of street players. Don't worry: you won't get stuck with your choices. You'll get many chances to replace these ballers later.

Proving Grounds

The Proving Grounds screen is where you do your planning. This screen includes:

- A list of courts where you can play
- Detailed info on the event happening on each court (highlight the court to read its info)
- Your current Rep and Street Points
- The day (important, as some events happen on specific days)

Court names are either black or grayed-out. Grayed-out courts are ones that you can't play on yet because your Rep is not high enough.

Time passes in Street Challenge; every game you play advances the clock. Some days offer tournaments or special events that you can participate in. Other days nothing special pops up, so you should just join one of the various pick-up games.

You can make time pass at the Proving Grounds screen by skipping a day. This is okay if you're impatient, but it's always best to play pick-up instead of skipping a day. Playing pick-up earns you Street 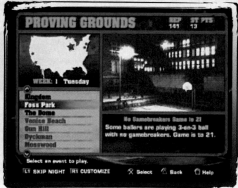 Points, which you can use to improve your baller and buy custom gear. Skipping a day earns you nothing.

Street Challenges

A variety of challenges await you on the street. They fall into three general categories: reputation-based challenges, special events (tournaments and dunk contests), and plain old pick-up.

Reputation-Based Challenges

These semi-random challenges pop up every once in awhile. A screen appears to inform you whenever they're available. Just go to the court where the challenge is happening to take part in it.

These challenges are always based on your Rep. Your Rep must be at a certain level for individual challenges to appear.

> **TIP?**
> Just play lots of pick-up games (and win!) to crank up your Rep. Don't worry about it; if you consistently win, it'll all fall into place.

Challenges can be any different game type (including Dunks Only, Trick Point Challenge, Old School Scoring, and all the rest). They often feature NBA players, so there's a big incentive to win and grab those players for your own team!

These one-off Street Challenges against NBA players are also triggered by your Rep. There are several throughout the duration of Street Challenge. Examples include the following:

Head-to-Head Trick Point Challenge

One of the NBA's best handles is playing some 3-on-3 basketball. It's a trick point challenge to 250,000 points!

Required Rep — 250

Street Point Bonus — None

Clothes Unlock — None

Think You're A Big Shot?

Your rival is calling you out at your home court. Only long range shots are going to count in this game. No Gamebreakers.

Required Rep — 400

Street Point Bonus — 250

Clothes Unlock — None

Rbk 3-on-3 Challenge 2

Three of Rbk's top ballers are playing together and taking on all comers here today.

Required Rep — 600

Street Point Bonus — 500

Clothes Unlock — Rbk S Carter BB II Wht / Blu

> ### Rivals
> Upgrade your team by picking up new blood and kicking out lesser talents. However, occasionally those lesser talents get ticked off that you discarded them and they become rivals. Rivals will sometimes challenge you to a game.
>
> You lose a lot of Rep for turning down a rival challenge. You may also lose a lot of Rep if you take it but are defeated. The bottom line: when confronted with a rival challenge, you'd better take it, and you'd better win!

Special Events (Tournaments & Dunk Contests)

Tournaments and dunk contests offer the chance to display your skills in a big way. Unlike challenges, which pop up semi-randomly, tournaments and dunk contests always happen on a particular date.

Tournaments sometimes have a minimum Rep requirement, but many have no Rep requirement at all. You do have to pay a few Street Points to register for a tournament, however. (Pay up; it's worth it.)

Dunk contests don't have minimum Rep requirements, and they don't charge admission fees. Just show up and throw down some nasty dunks!

These events happen on specific days, though, so they are sorted by the day they happen.

Additional information includes the registration fee required to enter tournaments (the cost is in Street Points) and the trophies or banners you can unlock by winning.

If several events happen on the same day, you must choose one.

You might notice the three tournaments on Day 70. The one you're allowed into depends on how well you've done in your Street Challenge, overall. The Grande Finale is the most prestigious tournament.

Unlocked banners may be placed on your custom court.

Tournaments & Dunk Contests

DAY	EVENT NAME	DESCRIPTION	EVENT TYPE	REG. FEE (SP)	REQUIRED REP	SP BONUS	CLOTHES UNLOCK	TROPHY	BANNER UNLOCK
4	Dunk Contest: Tandy Takeoff (happens every 2 weeks)	Dunk Contest tonight at the Tandy Center.	Dunk Contest	—	—	250	—	—	—
6	Streetball Royalty	The all-city tournament is going down in your hometown. Four squads will battle to see who comes out on top.	Tournament	50	—	500	—	—	City Name Black
7	EA SPORTS BIG™ Concrete Classic	The EA SPORTS BIG™ Concrete Classic 3-on-3 tournament is at The Hawk in Pittsburgh. 4 teams, single elimination.	Tournament	250	—	750	—	—	Concrete Hawk White
9	Biggie Littles is Back	A 4-team, single-elimination, 3-on-3 tournament at The Cage in NYC.	Tournament	100	200	500	—	—	The Cage Green
11	EA SPORTS BIG™ Concrete Classic	The EA SPORTS BIG™ Concrete Classic 3-on-3 tournament is at Gun Hill Playground. 4 teams, single elimination.	Tournament	250	—	500	—	—	Concrete Gun Hill Lt blue
13	Dunk Contest: Rucker Park	Eight competitors square off in a dunk contest at Rucker Park.	Dunk Contest	—	—	500	—	—	—
13	Street V3-On-3 Tournament	A 4-team, single-elimination tournament at Dyckman Park.	Tournament	150	—	750	—	—	V3On3 Dyckman

Tournaments & Dunk Contests (cont'd)

DAY	EVENT NAME	DESCRIPTION	EVENT TYPE	REG. FEE (SP)	REQUIRED REP	SP BONUS	CLOTHES UNLOCK	TROPHY	BANNER UNLOCK
13	Streetball Royalty	The all-city tournament is going down in your hometown. Four squads will battle to see who comes out on top.	Tournament	50	—	500	—	—	City Name Gold
14	Doing Big Things	Biggie Littles is favored to win another tournament at The Cage in NYC.	Tournament	100	200	500	—	—	The Cage Black
16	Rbk Invitational Tournament	A 4-team, single-elimination tournament at Rucker Park. Sponsored by Rbk.	Tournament	300	—	500	—	—	Rbk Rucker Green
18	Head 2 Head Dunk Contest 1	Think you have hops? One of the NBA's best is ready to face you in a head-to-head dunk contest.	Dunk Contest	—	—	100	New Orleans Hornets Hat	—	—
18	Can You Spare A Dime	Clash with Dime, the streetball diva, in a 4-team, single elimination tournament challenge.	Tournament	100	300	500	—	—	The Dome Gold
20	Dunk Contest: Venice Beach	Four high flyers will battle it out in a contest for slam dunk supremacy.	Dunk Contest	—	—	500	—	—	—
20	EA SPORTS™ Roundball Classic	Play against former Roundball Classic participants in a 4-team, double-elimination tournament at Foss Park	Tournament	250	400	750	EA Sports Roundball Jers	—	EA Foss Gold
23	Head 2 Head Dunk Contest 2	Think you can jump? One of the NBA's best is ready to take you on in a head-to-head dunk contest.	Dunk Contest	—	—	200	Milwaukee Bucks Hat	—	—
23	The Rbk Invitational	A 4-team, single-elimination tournament at Venice Beach. Sponsored by Rbk.	Tournament	300	—	500	Rbk ATR Clear Out	—	Rbk Venice
25	Dropped by Dime	Dime, the first lady of the asphalt office, is favored to win another tournament at The Dome in Baltimore.	Tournament	100	300	500	—	—	The Dome White
27	Takashi Returns	Takashi is back to make some noise. His squad is the top-seed in a 4-team, single-elimination tournament Venice Beach.	Tournament	100	400	500	—	—	Venice White

Tournaments & Dunk Contests (cont'd)

DAY	EVENT NAME	DESCRIPTION	EVENT TYPE	REG. FEE (SP)	REQUIRED REP	SP BONUS	CLOTHES UNLOCK	TROPHY	BANNER UNLOCK
28	Dunk Contest: St. Louis	Some of the area's highest flyers compete for slam dunk supremacy at the Tandy Center in St. Louis.	Dunk Contest	—	—	250	—	—	—
28	Head 2 Head Dunk Contest 3	Think you can fly? One of the NBA's best is ready to go head-to-head with you in a dunk contest.	Dunk Contest	—	—	300	Orlando Magic Hat	—	—
30	Dunk Contest: Rucker Park	Four competitors will take it to the air for the title at Rucker Park in NYC.	Dunk Contest	—	—	500	—	—	—
30	EA SPORTS BIG™ Concrete Classic	The EA SPORTS BIG™ Concrete Classic 3-on-3 tournament is at Brighton Beach in England. 4 teams, single elimination.	Tournament	250	—	500	Rbk Boulevard	—	Concrete Brighton Blue
32	The Rbk Invitational	A 4-team, single-elimination tournament at Rucker Park in NYC. Sponsored by Rbk.	Tournament	300	—	500	Rbk High Post (blk/red)	—	Rbk Rucker Green
34	Dunk Contest: Venice Beach	The West Coast's highest flyers are vying for slam dunk supremacy at Venice Beach.	Dunk Contest	—	—	250	—	—	—
34	EA SPORTS™ Roundball Classic	Play against former Roundball Classic participants in a 4-team, double-elimination tournament at Foss Park.	Tournament	250	500	750	EA Sports Roundball Jers	—	EA SPORTS 2 White
35	Head 2 Head Dunk Contest 4	Think you got hops? One of the NBA's best is ready to face you in a head-to-head dunk contest.	Dunk Contest	—	—	400	GS Warriors Hat	—	—
35	Hand of the Rising Sun	Takashi, the swat-machine, is favored to win another tournament at Venice Beach on the left coast.	Tournament	100	400	500	—	—	Venice Lt Blue
39	Big Kid on the Block	He's got a big frame and big game. See if you can take out Phat at his 4-team, single-elimination tournament at MacGregor Park.	Tournament	100	500	500	—	—	McGregor Blue
40	Head 2 Head Dunk Contest 5	Think you can fly? One of the NBA's best is ready to take you on in a head-to-head dunk contest.	Dunk Contest	—	—	500	Houston Rockets Hat	—	—
41	Street V3-On-3 Tournament	A 4-team, best of three tournament at Dyckman Park in NYC.	Tournament	150	—	750	—	—	V3On3 Dyckman

Tournaments & Dunk Contests (cont'd)

DAY	EVENT NAME	DESCRIPTION	EVENT TYPE	REG. FEE (SP)	REQUIRED REP	SP BONUS	CLOTHES UNLOCK	TROPHY	BANNER UNLOCK
42	Dunk Contest: Rbk Challenge	Take on seven of the biggest dunkers Rbk has to offer in a Dunk Contest at Rucker Park.	Dunk Contest	—	—	1000	Rbk ATR Pump (wht/blu/red)	Rbk Challenge	—
44	The Rbk Invitational	Go up against 3 teams of Reebok's best in a 4-team, round-robin tournament at Rucker Park. Sponsored by Rbk.	Tournament	300	—	1000	Rbk Question II (blk/blk)	—	Rbk Rucker Green
45	Dunk Contest: History Lesson Part 1	Compete against three of the greatest dunkers in NBA history at Venice Beach.	Dunk Contest	—	—	750	Rbk High Post (wht/red)	History Lesson 1	—
46	EA SPORTS BIG™ Concrete Classic	The EA SPORTS BIG™ Concrete Classic 3-On-3 tournament is at Gun Hill Playground in NYC. 8 teams, single elimination.	Tournament	250	—	500	Rbk Blacktop Pump	—	Concrete Gun Hill Lt Blue
46	5 Boroughs Tournament	The Beastie Boys are holding a 4-team, single-elimination tournament at Dyckman Park in NYC.	Tournament	100	—	750	—	—	—
47	Dunk Contest: New York	NYC is jumping as four big-time dunkers battle it out for the title.	Dunk Contest	—	—	250	—	New York	—
47	Texas-Sized Game	Phat, the big fella, is favored to win another tournament at MacGregor Park Pavilion.	Tournament	100	500	500	—	—	McGregor Lt Blue
48	Head 2 Head Dunk Contest 6	Think you can jump? One of the NBA's best is ready to face you in a head-to-head dunk contest.	Dunk Contest	—	—	600	LA Lakers Hat	—	—
48	Certified Bonafide	Bonafide's squad is favored to win this 4-team, single elimination tournament at Dyckman Park in NYC.	Tournament	100	650	500	—	—	Dyckman Blue
49	Dunk Contest: History Lesson Part 2	Take on three of the greatest dunkers in NBA history in a Dunk Contest at Tandy.	Dunk Contest	—	—	750	Rbk ATR 2nd Coming (wht/blu)	History Lesson 2	—
51	Street V3-On-3 Tournament.	A 4-team, best of three tournament at Dyckman Park in NYC.	Tournament	150	—	750	—	—	V3On3 Dyckman

Tournaments & Dunk Contests (cont'd)

DAY	EVENT NAME	DESCRIPTION	EVENT TYPE	REG. FEE (SP)	REQUIRED REP	SP BONUS	CLOTHES UNLOCK	TROPHY	BANNER UNLOCK
53	Dunk Contest: The Future of Flight	Go up against seven of the NBA's most explosive dunkers at Holcombe Rucker Park	Dunk Contest	—	—	1000	Rbk Answer 8 (wht/red)	Future of Flight	—
54	Head 2 Head Dunk Contest 7	Think you got hops? One of the NBA's best is ready to take you on in a head-to-head dunk contest.	Dunk Contest	—	—	700	New Jersey Nets Hat	—	—
54	The Undisputed	Bonafide still has the sick handles. His squad is favored to win another tournament at Dyckman Park in NYC.	Tournament	100	650	500	—	—	Dyckman Lt Blue
55	Dunk Contest: Legendary Status	Compete against seven of the greatest dunkers in NBA history at Rucker Park.	Dunk Contest	—	—	1000	Rbk Answer 8 (blk/blk)	Legendary Status	—
56	EA SPORTS BIG™ Roundball Classic	Play against former Roundball Classic participants in a 4-team, double-elimination tournament at Mosswood Park.	Tournament	250	750	100	EA Sports Roundball WU	—	EA Mosswood White
58	Respect Your Elders	Stretch is still holding it down, and his squad is favored to win this big tournament at Rucker Park in Harlem.	Tournament	100	700	500	—	—	Rucker Green
60	Head 2 Head Dunk Contest 8	Think you can soar? One of the NBA's best is ready to face you in a head-to-head dunk contest.	Dunk Contest	—	—	800	Cleveland Cavaliers Hat	—	—
63	Still Reigning	Stretch, the elder statesman of streetball, is favored to win another tournament at the Rucker in NYC.	Tournament	100	700	500	—	—	Rucker Red
70	Last Chance at Glory	An 8-team, single-elimination tournament at Foss Park in Chicago. Some talented ballers will show up here.	Tournament	—	—	2500	—	—	Street V3 Orange
70	The Big Finish	An 8-team, single-elimination tournament at Venice Beach. Some of the NBA's very best will be here.	Tournament	—	—	5000	—	—	Street V3 Gold
70	The Grande Finale	An 8-team, single-elimination tournament against some of the greatest players in NBA history. This is going to be big!	Tournament	—	—	10000	—	—	Street V3 Gold

Plain Old Pick-Up

You should participate in challenges, tournaments, and dunk contests whenever possible. But when nothing else is available, it's time to hit the playgrounds and play some basic pick-up ball. It may not be as glamorous as the other stuff, but it earns you vital Rep and Street Points.

Building the Perfect Baller

The centerpiece of your Street Challenge team is your created baller. He serves as captain and he's the only guy you can upgrade with Street Points. He also plays in every game. So it pays to put a little thought into him (or her) from the very start.

CHOOSE GENDER

Body Type and Stats

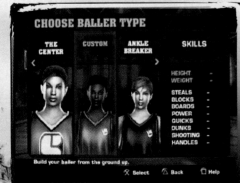

First, let's get one thing straight: body type (height and weight) affects how much it costs to buy skills, but it *doesn't affect the skills themselves.*

For example, you can make a seven-foot baller, but if you don't give him any shot-blocking ability, he won't be able to swat the rock. Similarly, you can have a fat baller who gets run over because his power stat is low, or a skinny baller who's slow despite his quick-looking body.

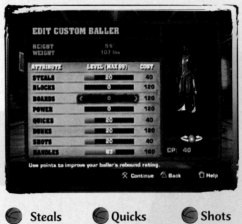

What body type *does* do is affect how much it *costs* to buy certain skills. For example, the shorter and skinnier your baller is, the cheaper the following skills are:

Steals   Quicks   Shots   Handles

On the other hand, these skills are cheaper for tall and heavy ballers:

Blocks   Boards   Power

The dunks skill is different, because it has an "ideal" height and weight. The ideal dunking height is 6'6". As a player gets farther away from that height, it costs more for him to buy the skill. The "ideal" dunking weight is between 230 and 240 pounds. Dunks cost progressively more as players get heavier or lighter than that.

The two "extreme" body types are tall and heavy, and short and skinny. Certain skills are very cheap for these body types, but others are very expensive. Most ballers fall somewhere in between these two extremes. Figure out ahead of time what skills you want your baller to possess, and then select a height and weight that make your desired skills cheap.

Height and Shot Blocking

We told you that height and weight don't directly affect player skills, but there is one exception. Height *does* have some effect on shot-blocking. A 5'10" baller with a 99 blocks rating and a 6'10" baller with the same rating will both be excellent shot-blockers, but the shorter one won't be able to reach a few balls that the taller one can. The effect of height is less than you might think, but it does exist. The moral of the story: if shot-blocking is in your baller's future, we recommend a height in the mid six-foot range or higher.

The cost to increase a skill also goes up as your baller gets better in that area.

Cost to Upgrade Skills

BALLER'S SKILL	COST TO UPGRADE
20 or less	Lowest
20–40	Medium
40–60	High
60–80	Very High
80–99	Highest

Since skills are very cheap until they hit 20, there's no reason not to give your baller at least 20 in every skill, early on in the Street Challenge.

Handler or Shot-Blocker?

When you first build a baller, it helps to know what sort of player you want. Eventually you'll earn enough Street Points to make your baller a well-rounded powerhouse, but at the start, he or she won't have a lot of points, so it's best to focus on a couple of key skills.

You can mold your baller any way you want, but here are two paths that we recommend.

Mad Handles Baller

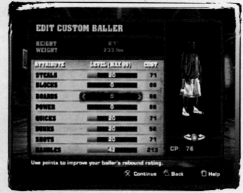

If you choose this route, focus on handles above all else. Steal ability should also be good. You won't have enough points to build up shooting or dunking abilities from the start, but that's okay. Work on them later.

When you do start to build up offensive skills, we recommend focusing on dunks over shots (unless you really love the long ball). If you decide to go the shooting route, really crank the shooting skill and make your baller a deadly sniper.

This baller will be more versatile if he or she is reasonably tall (in the six-foot range), but even a super-short baller can be effective in this role.

Force in the Middle

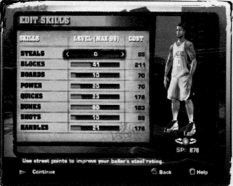

The other obvious route is to make a big-time shot-blocker. Crank up your player's height and blocks skill, and add in some dunks skill, too. Later on you will build these abilities up as high as they'll go and add in some power to help your player win those mid-air battles. A little handles might also be nice to avoid getting the ball stolen too frequently.

Our Reasoning

Our recommended ballers are focused on a couple of skills, instead of being good at everything for this reason: middle-of-the-road players with okay ability in several areas are common. Specialists are much harder to find, which is why it pays to build your own.

Also, specialized players are easy to play. That's because there's always a "right" way to approach things. For example, if you have a great shot-blocker, you *know* your defense should focus on blocks. If you have a baller who can steal, you *know* that steals and trick counters are your meal ticket. Playing a baller that's just okay in both areas leaves you confused about what to do—and not very effective.

We chose handles and blocks as our ballers' top skills because we think they're the most important skills in the game.

Ranking Player Skills

Not all player skills are equal. It's important to know which skills contribute most to success.

Handles and shot-blocking are probably the most important skills in the game. Handles is key not only because it lets you perform the best tricks, but also because it increases the chances of getting you open (by faking out opponents) and decreases the chances of getting the ball stolen (or your trick countered). Blocks are important because they can counter both long range shots and dunks, and it forces the opponent to think twice about every shot.

Steals and dunks are also very important. Steals allow you to grab the ball and score easy baskets. Steals also prevent opposing ball handlers from running wild and racking up monster trick points. Dunks are important for finishing combos and putting points on the board.

Power and shooting are somewhat less important, but you can tailor your game style to emphasize them. Powerful players sometimes run over weaker

Ranking Player Skills (cont'd)

opponents, so if you emphasize power, look for contact wherever possible. This is a game of stylish dunks, so shooting is not king—especially when the opponent can goaltend your shots. But the long range score is a deadly weapon if used properly, so your personal style might make shooting a priority.

Speed and rebounds are near the bottom of the skill barrel. You can compensate somewhat for slow player speed by thinking ahead and moving into position. Furthermore, if your slow guy is a shot-blocker, he can just goaltend, which doesn't require speed. Rebounding ability only comes into play when two players have a chance at a board. The fact of the matter is that shots and dunks usually go in (or are turbo blocked), so there are fewer loose balls than you might expect.

This is just our take on the skills; your mileage may vary. Hone your game to a fine edge, and you might find that your strategy emphasizes those "lower" skills.

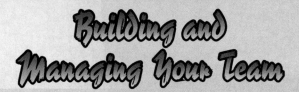

Building and Managing Your Team

The classic team in this game has three players with distinct roles: your point-guard style ball handler, your monstrous shot-blocker, and your high-octane scorer.

The ball handler tends to be short (but doesn't have to be), and has mad handles and steals. It helps if he's fairly quick and can shoot or dunk.

The shot-blocker is tall and strong, capable of swatting shots and throwing down big dunks. This player often has a good power rating.

The scorer is usually in the middle, size-wise (maybe 6'6" to 6'10") and has off-the-charts dunking ability. He might also be a good shooter, and it helps if he can handle (if only to avoid coughing up the ball). He might be able to steal, or block some shots, or both; he's a "do-it-all" type of guy.

Once you get skilled, feel free to go nuts and throw out the rules. Play a line of monstrous shot-blockers or an all-handles lineup. But when you're first getting started, stick with the basics to build an effective team.

Picking a Good Starting Team

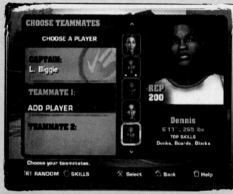

Your starting team should include the three player types discussed above (point guard, shot-blocker, scorer). Your created baller will be one of those guys, so pick two teammates who fill in the other roles.

When picking those first couple of teammates, a good rule of thumb is to check out their Rep. High Rep usually means good skills, so by looking at Rep you can quickly identify the best players.

Managing Your Custom Baller

Throughout most of the Street Challenge, your custom baller will be the *worst player on your team!* That's because you didn't start out with many Street Points to buy him abilities. Later on, as you start to

enhance his abilities, you'll also be picking up new teammates with improved skills—so your custom baller will continue to lag behind.

It would be nice if you could sit your custom baller on the bench, but he's the captain—so he must play. How should you deal with this?

The answer is to make your baller decent at just one thing. Start him out with decent shot-blocking or handles, and then park him down low or have him bring the ball up the court. Only let your baller do the one thing he's good at; let everyone else do all the rest.

Gradually build your baller up with Street Points, making him more competent. Let him do a little more each time you improve his skills. By the time you get deep into the Street Challenge, he'll be good enough that you don't have to worry about him anymore.

Adding Players

You play three ballers at a time, but your roster holds five. You fill those extra slots by cherry-picking the best players from defeated teams.

Later on, when all five slots are filled, you'll still be on the lookout for new talent. Whenever a defeated team has a baller that's better than someone on your team, you'll replace your mediocre player with the better one.

Early on in Street Challenge, you won't play teams that are particularly skilled. So you might be tempted to not take players from those teams, even if you have empty slots. Think again! Even if the defeated players aren't any better than your current guys, you should always carry a full five-man roster. Why? Because different challenges have different rules and you might want to put a different mix of players on the court.

For example, let's say you're going to play a Dunks Only game. Your custom baller, a seven-foot shot blocker, isn't good at dunks yet. Your primary handler, a short point guard type, can't dunk at all. In that case it's handy to have those extra guys on the roster. Swap out the handler and swap in a good dunker to give yourself more offensive options.

Customizing the Team by Event

We just touched on this point, but it's worth repeating: always play the guys that are best suited to the game type you're playing. Here are the events that demand substitutions:

Customize Your Team by Event	
EVENT	RECOMMENDED MOVES
Trick Point Challenge	Load up on handles, steals
Gamebreaker Wins	Load up on handles, steals
Dunks Only	Remove short guys, replace with dunkers
Old School Scoring	Replace shooters with dunkers

Morale

Your players may become disgusted and bolt if you lose too much or if they don't get enough playing time. Don't worry too much about this; just play well and win and you've got half the battle won.

If a player leaves because you weren't giving him enough playing time, it's probably not a big deal. If he was your best player you'd have put him on the court more! Still, if you want to retain players in the future, try to mix up the types of events you play and mix up your lineup accordingly from one game to the next.

Scoring points quickly is the name of the game in *NBA STREET V3*. This chapter explains the intricacies of Street offense and helps you fine-tune your game, whether you're playing a Street Challenge or a pickup game against your friends.

Game Overview

The rules in this game can change. For example, you might play an "old school" game where all shots score one point (regardless of range) or an NBA rules game (where short shots are worth two points and long-range shots are worth three).

You accumulate trick points as you play. If enough trick points build up, you get a chance to shoot a Gamebreaker, which gives you points and subtracts points from the opponent's score.

Sometimes you'll play games where the score doesn't matter; the winner in these games is the team that gets the most trick points first.

> **TIPP**
> It is possible to win a standard game by completely ignoring trick points and just concentrating on scoring, but it's tough due to the point swings caused by Gamebreakers.

Tricks

Tricks are divided into *tiers*, or levels. Each tier is named for the number of turbo buttons required to perform the trick. So for example, a Tier 0 trick doesn't require any turbo buttons at all. Just press the trick button or trick stick by itself to do a Tier 0 trick. As you might expect, pressing two turbo buttons and the trick stick results in a Tier 2 trick.

Why Do Tricks?

Tricks serve two purposes. First, all tricks give you trick points. Second, a trick can make your defender fall down, stumble, or otherwise get out of your way.

Higher-tier tricks use more turbo and give you more trick points. They are also harder to perform than lower-tier tricks.

Defenders only get faked out if they're close to you when you perform the trick. Drive into them before starting the trick to maximize the chances of faking them out.

The tier of a trick does *not* affect how likely it is to fake out a defender. Tier only affects how many trick points you receive for successfully performing the trick.

> **TIPP**
> In a game played for trick points instead of points, your only goal is to accumulate trick points. In these cases you'll want to use the whole shot clock doing tricks.

What Gives Trick Points?

You get points for doing tricks, obviously. But you also get trick points for shots, dunks, alley-oops, blocks, steals, picks, hook-ups, and rebounds. Any skillful play will net you trick points.

Trick Combos

Combos are simply chains of moves that yield trick points. Any time you get trick points (even for stuff like rebounds, blocks, or steals), you have about three seconds to do something *else* that gives you
trick points. Keep doing stuff that gives you trick points in rapid succession, and then finish it all off with a score (a basket, dunk, or alley-oop). You then get bonus points for a trick combo.

The more tricks and moves you string together, the bigger the combo and the more trick points you win. Just remember that you must keep doing moves within about three seconds of each other or you lose the combo effect. And, you only score the combo if you score a basket.

Who Can Do Tricks?

High-tier tricks give lots of trick points, but they're also tough to perform. Only players with good handles should try the toughest tricks.

The following tables show how much handles is recommended for each trick tier. You'll notice that the tiers are different on the different consoles; that's because there are four turbo buttons on the PS2, but only three on the other consoles. We explain this in more detail in the next section.

Trick Tier Guidelines on PlayStation® 2	
TRICK TIER	RECOMMENDED HANDLES
Tier 0	Everyone can do these
Tier 1	Everyone can do these
Tier 2	40 Handles
Tier 3	60 Handles
Tier 4	80 Handles

Trick Tier Guidelines on Xbox® and GameCube™	
TRICK TIER	RECOMMENDED HANDLES
Tier 0	Everyone can do these
Tier 1	40 Handles
Tier 2	60 Handles
Tier 3	80 Handles

If you try a trick that's beyond a player's capability, he is likely to screw it up, fall down, and cough up the ball. The bottom line: know your players' handles abilities and don't attempt tricks that they should not do.

Trick Chapters and Trick Books

Tricks are divided into three Chapters. When you first start the game, you automatically perform only Chapter One tricks. By successfully using a particular Chapter One trick in a combo, you unlock the equivalent Chapter Two trick.

To perform Chapter Two tricks, open the Trick Book for your created baller (or the default Trick Book if you want to alter the moves that everyone else uses). In the Trick Book you can specify which Chapter trick your baller will perform every time you press a certain combination of the trick stick and turbo buttons.

Successfully do a Chapter Two trick in a combo to unlock the Chapter Three trick. Then you may select that trick in the Trick Book, also.

What's the difference between Chapter One, Two, and Three tricks? Just their look, name, and style. Chapter Three tricks are no more and no less effective than Chapter One tricks. So just pick the moves you like best for your Trick Book.

Trick List

You'll notice that some tricks only exist for the PS2. That's because the PS2 version of this game has four turbo buttons, while the Xbox and GameCube versions have only three. As a result, the PS2 has an extra tier of tricks; this bottom tier of tricks does not happen on the Xbox or GameCube.

Remember that only a trick's tier (turbo level) affects how many points you get for pulling it off. So the difference between individual tricks on each tier is simply *style*.

The following tables list every trick in the game.

PS2-Only Tricks (Tier 0)

PS2	CHAPTER 1 TRICK	CHAPTER 2 TRICK	CHAPTER 3 TRICK
⇓	Two-Time	The Setup	Heads Up
⇘	Roll On	Two Step	Back Track
⇒	Reel2Reel	Criss-Cross	Funknflash
⇗	That's a Wrap	Breakin' You Off	Yo-Yo
⇑	Off the Chain	Inside Out	Crossed Out
⇖	No Hands	Step Daddy	Fools Gold
⇐	Left Ya	Flexnflow	Spinoff
⇙	Through the Cut	Gone Fishin'	Smooth Groove

In the following tables 1T, 2T, 3T, and 4T denotes 1 Turbo, 2 Turbos, 3 Turbos, etc.

Basic Tricks (Tier 0 on GameCube and Xbox, Tier 1 on PS2)

PS2	XBOX	GAME-CUBE	CHAPTER 1 TRICK	CHAPTER 2 TRICK	CHAPTER 3 TRICK
1T+⇓	Ⓡ	Ⓒ	Off the Hook	Downshift	Step Show
1T+⇘	Ⓡ	Ⓒ	The Grampa	Da Treadmill	Good Foot
1T+⇒	Ⓡ	Ⓒ	Cook' Em	Hurricane	Mind Bender
1T+⇗	Ⓡ	Ⓒ	Psyche	Brotha Please	Shammgod
1T+⇑	Ⓡ	Ⓒ	Cha Cha	Underbelly	Double Cross
1T+⇖	Ⓡ	Ⓒ	Immobilize	Cyclone	Drop the Needle
1T+⇐	Ⓡ	Ⓒ	Change Up	Shimmie Sham	Subway Car
1T+⇙	Ⓡ	Ⓒ	On the Prowl	Street Shuffle	Y2 Next

Intermediate Tricks (Tier 1 on GameCube and Xbox, Tier 2 on PS2)

PS2	XBOX	GAME-CUBE	CHAPTER 1 TRICK	CHAPTER 2 TRICK	CHAPTER 3 TRICK
2T+↓	1T+Ⓡ	1T+Ⓒ	All Good	Back to the Lab	Street Wise
2T+↘	1T+Ⓡ	1T+Ⓒ	Double Dutch	Steady Rockin'	Sweet N' Sour
2T+→	1T+Ⓡ	1T+Ⓒ	Through the Basement	Breakin' Ankles	Move N' Groove
2T+↗	1T+Ⓡ	1T+Ⓒ	Throwback	Non-Fiction	Spin Cycle
2T+↑	1T+Ⓡ	1T+Ⓒ	Turn Style	Fro Fake	Spinner
2T+↖	1T+Ⓡ	1T+Ⓒ	Left No Right	Hopscotch	Appetizer
2T+←	1T+Ⓡ	1T+Ⓒ	Farmer's Market	Clowning Around	Below the Belt
2T+↙	1T+Ⓡ	1T+Ⓒ	Hypnotizer	The Heza	Thin Man

Advanced Tricks (Tier 2 on GameCube and Xbox, Tier 3 on PS2)

PS2	XBOX	GAME-CUBE	CHAPTER 1 TRICK	CHAPTER 2 TRICK	CHAPTER 3 TRICK
3T+↓	2T+Ⓡ	2T+Ⓒ	Side Order Of Cheese	Playin' Celo	Gator Walk
3T+↘	2T+Ⓡ	2T+Ⓒ	Ain't No Thang	Look Both Ways	Street Legal
3T+→	2T+Ⓡ	2T+Ⓒ	Top Spin	Hypnotic	Cheese Fries
3T+↗	2T+Ⓡ	2T+Ⓒ	Look Ma	Hide and Go Seek	Chopper Down
3T+↑	2T+Ⓡ	2T+Ⓒ	Made Ja Reach	Hot Buttered Popcorn	Tummy Ache
3T+↖	2T+Ⓡ	2T+Ⓒ	Smoke Screen	Backspin	Yo Yo Sick
3T+←	2T+Ⓡ	2T+Ⓒ	Left Behind	Chrome Dome	Saturn Rings
3T+↙	2T+Ⓡ	2T+Ⓒ	Windmill Skate	Back At Me	Trick or Treat

Ultimate Tricks (Tier 3 on GameCube and Xbox, Tier 4 on PS2)

PS2	XBOX	GAME-CUBE	CHAPTER 1 TRICK	CHAPTER 2 TRICK	CHAPTER 3 TRICK
4T+↓	3T+Ⓡ	3T+Ⓒ	Marinate'n	Bakin' Biscuits	On da Low Low
4T+↘	3T+Ⓡ	3T+Ⓒ	Roll Out	Slip N' Slide	Head Banger
4T+→	3T+Ⓡ	3T+Ⓒ	Check Yo Bags	Helicopter	Getting Krunk
4T+↗	3T+Ⓡ	3T+Ⓒ	Magic	Heads or Tails	Fo Shizzle
4T+↑	3T+Ⓡ	3T+Ⓒ	Home Remedy	Cartwheel	The Pistol
4T+↖	3T+Ⓡ	3T+Ⓒ	Biggie Little	Pancakin'	Droppin' Dimes
4T+←	3T+Ⓡ	3T+Ⓒ	Tornado	Gotcha Open	Shimmie Sham Bam
4T+↙	3T+Ⓡ	3T+Ⓒ	Kick It Ova Heea	Hip Drop	Osmosis

Trick Passes

Trick passes, such as Off the Heezay and Back 2 Papa, score lots of trick points (especially in combos with vicious dunks). Don't try these passes with just anyone; have your best handles player do them, especially when facing a player with weak handles. Trick passes can be countered, so be careful.

Trick passes might seem a little tough at first, because you must *stop moving* to do them. In a fast-moving game, it's hard to come to a complete stop. Also, if you stop for too long, your opponent can anticipate the trick pass and counter it. You must master the art of stopping and doing the pass *quickly*.

You must be in the right position to do trick passes. Off the Heezay, Bootay, Back, and Footay only work if your defender is quite close. Similarly, you must face the basket to do a Back 2 Papa, and it's tough if you aren't at least across the half-court line.

Practice trick passes and work them into your combos. A combo that includes a high-level trick and a trick pass, finished by a top-tier dunk, fills up your Gamebreaker meter in no time.

Shots and Dunks

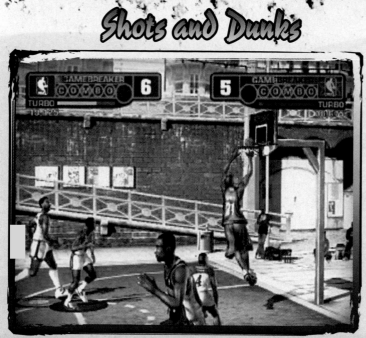

As important as tricks are, shots and dunks are how you score your points—so you can't ignore 'em. Here's an in-depth look at shots and dunks.

Making Your Shots Fall

Most of the time you want to dunk rather than shoot. However, there are definitely times when a shot is better. Long-range shots score extra points, and switching to a shot or layup instead of a dunk sometimes prevents you from getting blocked.

Here are some tips for increasing your shooting percentages:

- Use players with a high shooting rating
- Release the shot button just before the top of your jump
- Get close to the basket (or close to the three-point line for long-range shots)
- Shoot when nobody is close to you (you're wide open)
- Pump fake to draw your defender into the air; often this is just as good as getting wide open.

Those last two points are important. Your shooting percentage is affected when someone's in your face, even if he or she isn't quite in position to block your shot. You'll do better if you shoot while wide-open, or at least pump fake to ensure that your defender isn't jumping at the same time you are.

Dunk List

Like tricks, dunks have several tiers. Unlike tricks, you can't specify which dunk to perform. You just specify a tier by pressing a certain number of turbos and your player randomly performs a dunk from that tier.

Because there are only three turbo buttons on the Xbox and GameCube, the Tier 0 and 1 dunks get mashed together. Doing a no-turbo dunk on the Xbox or GameCube randomly performs either a Tier 0 or Tier 1 dunk.

Tier 0 Dunks (No Turbo Buttons on All Platforms)

Light House	Jurassic	Double Dip
Mashed It	Night Train	Sidewinder
Rise & Shine	Crunch	

Tier 1 Dunks (1 Turbo on PS2, No Turbo on Xbox and GameCube)

Skyscraper	Monster Mash	Deodorant Stick
All That	Jungle Jam	Flush
Raise Yo Hands	Powerhouse	Way Back

Tier 2 Dunks (2 Turbos on PS2, 1 Turbo on Xbox and GameCube)

Put It Home	Look Out Below	Special Delivery
Spin da LP	Hangtime	Shockwave
Around the Way	Take That	Superfly
Around the World	Jet Stream	Two Scoops
Da Hangman	Backbreaker	Rock da Cradle
Booyah!	Ozone	Air Tight
Seismic		

Tier 3 Dunks (3 Turbos on PS2, 2 Turbos on Xbox and GameCube)

The Doctor	R.T.D.	Air Time
Buckdown	Mamma Jamma	Honey Dip
Air Raid	Dunkalicious	The Hammer
Jam City	Hammerdown	Wake Up Call
Stretch	Boomdown	Goin' Dolo
Bonafide	Remix	Through Wit It
Groundshaker	Shoulder Press	

Tier 4 Dunks (4 Turbos on PS2, 3 Turbos on Xbox and GameCube)

Dinner's Served	Nerve Damage	Flamboastin'
Flossin'	Krunk Junk	

All Tier 4 dunks are off-the-backboard dunks—in other words, you'll bounce the ball off the backboard and back to yourself as you do the dunk. Be sure that you're running straight toward the basket (not at an angle) before trying these, or you'll throw the ball away.

Gamebreakers and Dunk Contest Dunks

Gamebreaker dunks are completely different from normal dunks. You don't have much control over normal dunks, but you have *complete* control over a Gamebreaker. You can perform multiple tricks in midair, racking up mad trick points and affecting the point swing of the Gamebreaker. You can perform multiple tricks in midair when performing Gamebreakers or Dunk Contest dunks. Keep tapping the trick stick in different directions (with or without turbo button) to keep doing new tricks. Just be sure to stop before you reach the rim, or you'll miss your dunk!

Dunk Contest dunks are essentially just Gamebreakers, with a few extra options thrown in. Perform the trickiest possible dunk to gain maximum trick points and win the contest.

MASTER THE GAME

Want to build a Gamebreaker in one combo? Perform two tricks on your opponent around the center line, then quickly step up and fire a Back 2 Papa pass off the backboard. When the ball returns to your hand, perform an Off The Heezay pass and take it home for a dunk. Your opponent won't know what hit him and you'll have earned a Gamebreaker in a single combo!

Gamebreaker Hook-Ups and Crash Landings

Do tricks in midair until your player gets near the hoop. At that point, if a teammate has jumped into the air, press the pass button to hook him up.

Now do tricks with that player until he's near the hoop. If your third teammate has leaped into the air, press the pass button to hook him up, and do tricks with him.

When your final player is getting close to the hoop, let up on the trick stick and *stop doing tricks*. If you're in the process of doing a trick as your player reaches the hoop, he will crash land and the Gamebreaker is canceled.

Gamebreaker and Dunk Contest Tips

- You don't get maximum points for doing the same midair trick over and over. Do a multitude of different tricks.

- Remember to use turbos for your Gamebreaker and Dunk Contest tricks. High-turbo tricks take longer to do but score more points.

- Don't start a Gamebreaker dunk unless all three of your team members are inside the three-point line. If they aren't, they won't get involved in the Gamebreaker.

- Do multi-turbo tricks when you're high in the air, then switch to easy tricks as you approach the hoop to avoid crashing.

- Don't get greedy. It's better to stop doing tricks a little early than to bite off more than you can chew, then crash and get no points at all.

- Dunk Contests allow you to use props for higher trick point awards. These are just obstacles that you mustn't run into.

- To score big points in a Dunk Contest, always start with a Pass to Self move (covered later).

- You have 45 seconds to perform a Gamebreaker once the light changes color. That's more than enough time unless you commit turnovers.

Point Swing

A successful Gamebreaker always takes one point away from the opponent and gives you two, three, or four points. The number of points you gain depends on how many trick points you earned during the Gamebreaker dunk.

TIP!

It's easy to get a three-point Gamebreaker, but hard to get a four-point Gamebreaker. Our recipe for getting four-point Gamebreakers is to have the first dunker do top-tier tricks, the second dunker do medium-tier tricks, and the last dunker get spastic with a flurry of low-tier (no turbo) tricks. We do low-tier tricks last because they don't take long, so it's easy to stop and avoid a crash landing.

Gamebreaker Shots

A Gamebreaker shot (as opposed to a Gamebreaker dunk) always gives you the minimum point bonus (two points).

Gamebreaker shots have an extremely high chance of going in. If you use a decent shooter and shoot from anywhere closer than half-court, the shot is nearly automatic. Shooting with a lousy marksman or firing from beyond the half-court line drastically reduces the Gamebreaker's chances of going in.

Gamebreakers can be blocked, just like any other shot. So be careful if your opponent is in position to goaltend.

Gamebreaker and Dunk Contest Midair Tricks

PS2-Only Dunk Tricks (PS2 Tier 0)

TRICK	PS2	XBOX	GAMECUBE
Double Pump Waist High	⇓	—	—
Tap Outside Right Foot	⇘	—	—
Statue of Liberty Right	⇒	—	—
Right Hand Mailman	⇗	—	—
Double Pump Chest High	⇑	—	—
Left Hand Mailman	⇖	—	—
Statue of Liberty Left	⇐	—	—
Tap Outside Left Foot	⇙	—	—

Basic Dunk Tricks (PS2 Tier 1, Xbox and GameCube Tier 0)

TRICK	PS2	XBOX	GAMECUBE
Hold With Knees	1T+⇓	®↓	©↓
Tap Right Knee	1T+⇘	®↘	©↘
Liberty Spin Right	1T+⇒	®→	©→
Cover Your Eyes Right	1T+⇗	®↗	©↗
Windmill	1T+⇑	®↑	©↑
Cover Your Eyes Left	1T+⇖	®↖	©↖
Liberty Spin Left	1T+⇐	®←	©←
Tap Left Knee	1T+⇙	®↙	©↙

Intermediate Dunk Tricks (PS2 Tier 2, Xbox and GameCube Tier 1)

TRICK	PS2	XBOX	GAMECUBE
Double Pump	2T+⇓	1T+®↓	1T+©↓
Toss Under Right Arm	2T+⇘	1T+®↘	1T+©↘
Through Right Leg	2T+⇒	1T+®→	1T+©→
Tap Left Knee Right Knee	2T+⇗	1T+®↗	1T+©↗
Toss Behind Back Right	2T+⇑	1T+®↑	1T+©↑
Tap Right Knee Left Knee	2T+⇖	1T+®↖	1T+©↖
Through Left Leg	2T+⇐	1T+®←	1T+©←
Toss Under Left Arm	2T+⇙	1T+®↙	1T+©↙

Advanced Dunk Tricks (PS2 Tier 3, Xbox and GameCube Tier 2)

TRICK	PS2	XBOX	GAMECUBE
Behind Back Right	3T+⇓	2T+®↓	2T+©↓
Tap Inside Right Foot	3T+⇘	2T+®↘	2T+©↘
Shoulder Roll Right	3T+⇒	2T+®→	2T+©→
Around Head Right	3T+⇗	2T+®↗	2T+©↗
Behind the Back Left	3T+⇑	2T+®↑	2T+©↑
Around Head Left	3T+⇖	2T+®↖	2T+©↖
Shoulder Roll Left	3T+⇐	2T+®←	2T+©←
Tap Inside Left Foot	3T+⇙	2T+®↙	2T+©↙

Ultimate Dunk Tricks (PS2 Tier 4, Xbox and GameCube Tier 3)

TRICK	PS2	XBOX	GAMECUBE
Under Both Legs	4T+⇓	3T+®↓	3T+©↓
Through Both Legs Right	4T+⇘	3T+®↘	3T+©↘
Bounce Off Right Foot	4T+⇒	3T+®→	3T+©→
Bounce Off Right Knee	4T+⇗	3T+®↗	3T+©↗
Toss Behind Back Left	4T+⇑	3T+®↑	3T+©↑
Bounce Off Left Knee	4T+⇖	3T+®↖	3T+©↖
Bounce Off Left Foot	4T+⇐	3T+®←	3T+©←
Through Both Legs Left	4T+⇙	3T+®↙	3T+©↙

Dunk Contest-Only Controls and Moves

The midair tricks we just covered work both in Gamebreaker dunks and Dunk Contest dunks. But the following passes and takeoffs only work for Dunk Contest dunks.

Standard Takeoffs

The beginning of your dunk is called a takeoff. The most basic takeoffs are performed with the ball in your hands. You do *not* get any extra points for doing these takeoffs, so just use one that fits your personal style.

Dunk Contest Takeoffs (With the Ball)			
TAKEOFF STYLE	PS2	XBOX	GAMECUBE
Single Foot Takeoff (Straight Ahead)	●+L2	Ⓑ	Ⓑ
Double Foot Takeoff (Straight Ahead)	●+L2+R2	Ⓑ+Ⓛ+Ⓡ	Ⓑ+L+R
Single Foot Takeoff (180-Degree Rotation)	●+L1	Ⓑ+Ⓛ	Ⓑ+L
Double Foot Takeoff (180-Degree Rotation)	●+R1	Ⓑ+Ⓡ+ Click Ⓛ	Ⓑ+R+Z
Single Foot Takeoff (360-Degree Rotation)	●+R2	Ⓑ+Ⓡ	Ⓑ+R
Double Foot Takeoff (360-Degree Rotation)	●+R1+L1	Ⓑ+Ⓛ+ Click Ⓛ	Ⓑ+L+Z
Single Foot Takeoff (540-Degree Rotation)	●+R2+L1	Ⓑ+ Click Ⓛ	Ⓑ+Z
Single Foot Takeoff (720-Degree Rotation)	●+L2+R1	Ⓑ+Ⓛ+Ⓡ + Click Ⓛ	Ⓑ+L+ R+Z

Dunk Contest Passes to Self

The rule of thumb in Dunk Contests is the more "stuff" you do, the better your score. Standard takeoffs don't affect your score, because you have to take off *somehow*. However, you *can* boost your score by passing the ball into the air and then doing a takeoff without the ball.

Dunk Contest Passes to Self			
TAKEOFF STYLE	PS2	XBOX	GAMECUBE
Drop Kick off Backboard	L2+L1+ R2+R1+✕	Ⓛ+Ⓡ+Ⓐ	L+R+Ⓐ
Spinning Lob Kick	L1+L2+ R1+✕	Ⓛ+Ⓡ+ Ⓛ+Ⓐ	L+R+ Z+Ⓐ
Toss under Arm	L1+L2+R2+✕	—	—
Toss over Back	L1+R1+R2+✕	—	—
Off the Elbow to the Backboard	L2+R1+R2+✕	Ⓡ+Ⓐ	R+Ⓐ
Two Handed Lob	L2+L1+✕	—	—
Bounce between Legs off Backboard	L1+R1+✕	Ⓛ+Ⓐ	L+Ⓐ
Behind Back Kick	L1+R2+✕	Ⓡ+Ⓛ+Ⓐ	R+Z+Ⓐ
Behind Back off Backboard	L2+R1+✕	—	—
Behind Back off Ground	L2+R2+✕	Ⓐ	Ⓐ
Bounce off Knee Lob	R2+R1+✕	Ⓛ+Ⓛ+Ⓐ	L+Z+Ⓐ
Running Bounce off Ground	L1+✕	—	—

Dunk Contest Passes to Self (cont'd)			
TAKEOFF STYLE	PS2	XBOX	GAMECUBE
Underhand off Backboard	L2+X	—	—
Over Shoulder off Backboard	R1+X	—	—
Shot Lob	R2+X	L+A	Z+A

Takeoffs Without the Ball

Once you've done one of the "Pass to Self" moves, you need to jump without the ball, then hopefully catch it in midair so you can stuff it. Here's how to take off without the ball.

Dunk Contest Takeoffs (Without the Ball)			
TAKEOFF STYLE	PS2	XBOX	GAMECUBE
Single Foot Takeoff (Straight Ahead)	●+L2	B	B
Double Foot Takeoff (Straight Ahead)	●+L2+R2	B+L+R	B+L+R
Single Foot Takeoff (180-Degree Rotation)	●+L1	B+L	B+L
Double Foot Takeoff (180-Degree Rotation)	●+R1	B+R + Click L	B+R+Z

Dunk Contest Takeoffs (Without the Ball) (cont'd)			
TAKEOFF STYLE	PS2	XBOX	GAMECUBE
Single Foot Takeoff (360-Degree Rotation)	●+R2	B+R	B+R
Double Foot Takeoff (360-Degree Rotation)	●+R1+L1	B+L + Click L	B+L+Z
Single Foot Takeoff (540-Degree Rotation)	●+R2+L1	B+ Click L	B+Z
Single Foot Takeoff (720-Degree Rotation)	●+L2+R1	B+L+R + Click L	B+L+ R+Z

Props

The last things to consider in a Dunk Contest are props. Basically, props are just obstacles that you can grab and place on the court. They make your dunk harder, because you need to avoid them (or screw up the dunk).

Play around with props to get a feel for them. Here are the controls for placing props:

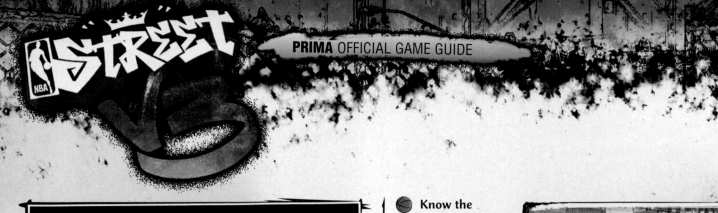

Dunk Contest Takeoffs

TAKEOFF STYLE	PS2	XBOX	GAMECUBE
Enable Prop Mode	SELECT	BLK	X
Highlight Prop/ Destination	D-Button or Left Analog Stick	L	◎
Select Prop/ Destination	✕	A	A
Remove Prop (If Prop on Court)	■	X	X

General Strategy

Finally, here are some tips that cover every aspect of the offensive game.

- If your turbo is dry, pump fake. It requires no turbo and often baits defenders into the air.

- If you have the shooters, don't forget long-range shots. A steady diet of two-pointers can sometimes defeat a high-flying dunking team—even if you fail to get any Gamebreakers.

- Call for picks. They knock your defender to the floor, leaving you with wide-open shot opportunities.

- In a multiplayer game, you can set your own picks whenever you don't have the ball. Press two turbos and the "Call for Pick" button simultaneously.

- Perform tricks whenever you're wide-open. Those are the easiest trick points you'll ever get!

- Know the handles and dunking skills of each player and only do tricks or dunks that are within that player's abilities.

- Keep your eyes open for high-leaping teammates while you're on the perimeter. Pass immediately to score the alley-oop.

- Keep your eyes open for leaping teammates while you're dunking. Pass to them for a high-scoring hook-up.

- Manage your turbo. Don't waste turbo going down the floor, if possible. Save it for tricks.

- Finish strong. It's better to do a couple of low-level tricks and finish with a high-tier dunk, than to do high-tier tricks and finish with a weak dunk or layup.

- Gamebreaker dunks are better than Gamebreaker shots. The exception is if your 45 seconds is almost up. In that case, just take a quick shot so you don't miss out on the Gamebreaker.

MASTER THE GAME

Want to cause the ultimate embarrassment to your opponent? Perform a Tier 3 trick (PS2) / Tier 2 trick (XBOX / GC) close to your opponent. (The "Smoke Screen" trick is particularly effective; these tricks are designed to turn your opponent around in confusion.) Then perform an Off The Bootay pass when they're looking the other way.

ADVANCED DEFENSE

There's an art to defense in *NBA STREET V3*, but its charm lies in its simplicity. There aren't many defensive moves to remember, so it's just a matter of using the right ones at the right times.

Steals and Trick Counters

Steals and trick counters are your main weapons when the ball is in your opponent's hands. Understanding how and when to use them will make you a good defensive player.

Stealing Facts

Here are some important facts about steals:

- Steal attempts use a little turbo, even though you don't press a turbo button to steal.
- A successful steal often pokes the ball loose, so be ready to dive for it.
- Your player's steal rating and the opponent's handles rating affect your chances of success.
- Your steal chances are best when the ball is waist high.
- Stealing works best if you *aren't moving*. You can still steal if your player is moving, but it's less likely to work.
- You can sometimes get a steal just by being in the passing lanes.

Stealing Technique

Armed with the facts we just presented, you're ready to improve your stealing technique. Here are our recommendations:

- Swipe freely when you're between the offensive player and the basket. But don't get carried away, or your opponent will blow right past you for an easy dunk, while you're still standing there swiping.
- Watch the ball, not the player. Swipe at the ball when it's at the top of its bounce.
- Anticipate where your opponent wants to go and move there; then let go of the movement stick before attempting your steal. (Remember that steals work best when you aren't moving.)
- Don't bother with steals if you're controlling a big, clumsy guy and you're defending a fast guard with good handles. Stay back a little and look for a block instead. Or switch to someone with good steal ability.
- Always try to steal from the opponent's big guys. They almost never have great handles.
- You can often get a steal just as your opponent finishes a trick. Wait until the precise instant the trick is completed, then swipe at the ball.

Trick Counter Facts

- As with steals, your chance of success depends on your steal ability and your opponent's handles.
- Trick counters work best if you do them right when your opponent begins his trick.

- As the trick progresses, you can still counter it, but your chances drop off. Your best bet is to counter a trick *early*.

- The tier of the trick being performed does *not* affect how difficult it is to counter—all tricks are equally hard to counter.

- Trick counters work on trick passes (like Off the Heezay) as well as standard tricks.

Trick Counter Technique

- Trick countering is all about guessing. Anticipate when your opponent is likely to spring a move on you, rather than simply reacting.

- Get in position and stand still while trick countering. As with steals, trick counters work best when you're motionless.

- Use someone with high steal ability to do most of your trick counters.

- A big guy near the basket will often try a simple trick to get open for a dunk. Be prepared to counter that trick and take the ball away.

- Human opponents often get into a rhythm or pattern with their tricks. Be aware of that pattern and you can anticipate when a trick is coming (and counter it).

- If your opponent is well into a trick, don't try to counter it. Wait until the end and try to steal instead.

- The offensive player must briefly stop moving to perform trick passes such as Off the Heezay. Be prepared for this and counter immediately when the ball handler stops.

The Art of Standing Still

In a game of constant motion, standing still may be the hardest lesson of all. But it's vital, both on offense and defense.

On offense, trick passes only work if you're not moving. Shots are somewhat more accurate if you stop before you fire.

On defense, standing still is even more crucial. Learn to get into position and stop before you try for a steal or trick counter. Your chances of success are *greatly* increased when you're motionless.

Standing still also helps with position defense. Your baller is harder to drive around if he's squarely in the offensive player's way and—you guessed it—standing still.

The moral of the story: get into position early and stop, rather than constantly running. You'll be amazed at how much this simple technique helps your game.

Blocks

Steals and trick counters are your weapons while the ball is on the court. When it's in the air, blocks are your only remaining option.

Blocking is an important skill. You'll usually want at least one good shot blocker on your team, even if it means overlooking players with other useful skills.

Goaltending (swatting the ball on the way down) is legal in *NBA STREET V3*, so parking a big guy near the basket and goaltending shots is a perfectly legitimate strategy. You can also stick close to your man and try to block at

the point of attack. You'll develop your own favorite strategies as you play.

Blocking Facts

- Hold down two turbos while blocking to turbo block and rip the ball out of the air.

- Goaltending is effective, but it's not guaranteed to work. Your blocking skill (and some randomness) affect your chances of success.

- If you played *NBA STREET Vol. 2*, note that goaltending is slightly less effective in this game.

- Taller players (naturally) have an advantage over shorter ones when blocking shots, but a short player can be an excellent shot blocker. It just requires good timing on your jumps.

- You can block dunks as well as shots.

- If two players meet in midair as one tries to dunk and the other tries to block, their strength ratings may come into play. The stronger player may knock down the weaker one. In this case, shot blocking ability becomes irrelevant!

- It's tough to block someone from behind, but it's definitely possible—especially if you have a good shot blocker.

- You can block Gamebreaker shots, but not Gamebreaker dunks. Once a Gamebreaker dunk is initiated, you just have to sit back and watch.

- The various dunk tiers are all equally hard to block (in other words, dunk tier does not factor into blocks).

Blocking Technique

- When goaltending, don't stand directly under the basket. Patrol an imaginary arc a few feet away from the basket, and swat the ball at that distance.

- If you choose to guard your man straight up and try to block shots as he releases, don't bite on ball fakes. Wait to see his feet leave the floor before jumping to block.

- Blocking is easiest if you're already in position and you jump in place, rather than jumping sideways.

- Always turbo block, if possible. It gives you instant possession of the ball.

- If your blocker has great strength, meet your opponent in the air and knock him down. If you have poor strength, avoid contact.

- Don't ignore the players that don't have the ball. If one of them jumps high for an alley-oop, get in his path and jump to block. You can foil alley-oops this way.

Position Defense

The last type of defense is position defense.

Position defense is not a specific move. Instead, it's a set of guidelines on where to stand in relation to your opponent. Here are some tips for good position defense.

🏀 Get right up on big guys if they get the ball in the paint and try to steal from them before they make their move.

🏀 Watch the shot clock; adjust your position based on the clock and your opponent. For example, if you're facing a poor-shooting team and the shot clock is near zero, back off and dare them to shoot. Don't give up a drive.

🏀 Stay between your man and the basket. Don't get too close and constantly chase him, or he'll get around you and beat you to the rack.

🏀 The slower your player (and faster the opponent), the more room you should give your opponent.

🏀 Move up close to swipe at the ball or counter a trick, then back off slightly. Standing too close allows your opponent to blow by you or knock you down with a trick.

🏀 Know your defensive player's capabilities. If your guy can't steal, play off even farther than usual and go for blocks. If your guy can't block, play closer.

TEAMS

This chapter covers every team and lists stats for every NBA player in the game (save for Legends, who appear in the next chapter).

Complete stats are given for every player: shooting, dunks, boards…all the important ratings are here. Also, look for recommended lineups and tips on winning with (and defeating) each team.

Most player stats are self-explanatory and were discussed in earlier chapters. "Number" is simply the player's jersey number (*not* a stat!) and "Grand Total" is the total of all player stats added together. The result is usually between the mid 300s and low 600s.

TIP?

The Grand Total stat is fun to look at, but it's deceptive; it's not the last word on how useful a player is. Instead, it's a measure of how well-rounded a player is. A baller with a high Grand Total is skilled in many areas, but you'll sometimes prefer a player with a lower Grand Total who's excellent in just a few specific (and important) skills. So take the Grand Total with a grain of salt.

ATLANTA HAWKS

PLAYERS

NAME	NUMBER	SHOTS	DUNKS	BOARDS	POWER	BLOCKS	STEALS	HANDLES	QUICKS	GRAND TOTAL
ANTOINE WALKER	8	70	60	70	70	35	60	70	60	503
AL HARRINGTON	3	60	75	75	75	25	55	60	70	501
KENNY ANDERSON	12	70	5	5	35	3	64	85	75	354
JOSH CHILDRESS	1	80	65	60	40	65	45	60	60	478
JON BARRY	20	80	15	45	45	25	75	75	70	453

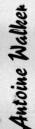

Antoine Walker

Best known from his days with the Celtics, Antoine Walker has the most general-purpose skills of any Hawks player. This makes him a very good mid-sized "utility" guy who can do a little of everything—handle, steal, board, dunk, you name it.

SUGGESTED LINEUP

- Al Harrington (offensive firepower, boards)
- Antoine Walker (firepower, all-around game)
- Josh Childress (blocks)

Al Harrington

Al Harrington is a quality offensive player and rebounder, and he's fast to boot. His dunking ability is tops on the Hawks, and in a game about dunks, that's a great reason to include him.

Kenny Anderson

Kenny Anderson is a competent point guard with above-average handles. His overall point total looks weak, but that just means he's specialized: don't expect blocks or boards. He's a good choice if you love high-difficulty tricks.

Josh Childress

Josh Childress is the Hawks' only credible shot-blocker, so he should be in the lineup (unless your strategy doesn't require blocks). His shot is surprisingly pure, making him an excellent long-range bomber.

Jon Barry

A fierce, well-traveled competitor, Barry is a good choice as your main ball handler. The fact that he can shoot lights-out doesn't hurt.

BEING

You've got some tough choices to make when playing the Hawks. There's no clear-cut starting lineup, no must-play crew that *has* to be on the court. It's all a matter of how you want to play it.

We recommend a big lineup with Harrington and Walker as your two offensive studs, and Josh Childress blocking shots down low. This lineup sacrifices a bit of handling for dunking and gunnery, resulting in an offensive-minded team that can really finish. Run and gun, focusing on middle-difficulty tricks and jams. Childress can fire the long-range shot if you fall behind. You won't stifle anyone with your D, so focus on the offensive fireworks.

DEFEATING

The Hawks aren't strong on D; even with Childress in the game, this team won't reject many shots. Load up on tricks and hammer the lanes hard, especially with your power guys. If they sag in to protect the lane, hoist threes. Don't let 'em off easy with low-value shots.

Defensively, you should play fairly close to your man. This is a better shooting team than dunking team, so you don't want to give up uncontested shots.

PLAYERS

NAME	NUMBER	SHOTS	DUNKS	BOARDS	POWER	BLOCKS	STEALS	HANDLES	QUICKS	GRAND TOTAL
PAUL PIERCE	34	85	75	55	65	30	75	75	75	569
RAEF LAFRENTZ	45	71	70	65	70	65	21	40	55	505
GARY PAYTON	20	80	21	35	45	21	75	90	75	462
RICKY DAVIS	12	60	80	40	50	21	60	70	80	473
MARK BLOUNT	30	80	70	75	70	65	55	50	65	563

Paul Pierce

Paul Pierce is an All-Star with a sweet shot and a great all-around game. Short of blocks, this man can do everything. He must be on the floor if you pick the Celtics.

SUGGESTED LINEUP

- Paul Pierce (all-around greatness)
- Gary Payton (great defense, mad handles)
- Mark Blount (blocks, boards, overall game)

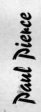

Raef LaFrentz

This Kansas alumnus is a solid player who can get you blocks and boards, as well as throw down a dunk. However, unless you're going for a big, block-oriented lineup, you'll usually take Mark Blount instead.

Gary Payton

The longtime Sonic has some of the best handles in the business, and his defense (think steals) is just as legendary as his trash-talking. He's a clear-cut choice at guard.

Ricky Davis

Ricky Davis combines good guard skills with a truly wicked dunking ability. Stick him in the lineup if you want to gear up on offense at the expense of a bit of defensive prowess.

Mark Blount

Mark Blount is a great choice for a Celtics big man. His blocking ability combined with power, dunking, and a surprising touch for shooting make him a great all-around choice. He's not just a defensive specialist!

BEING

The suggested lineup is a potent mix of high-flying offense and solid defense. All three guys can flat-out shoot—and the dunks ain't bad, either. Let Pierce carry the load on O, but don't be afraid to mix it up a little if the defense keys on him. Drive the lane with Pierce and kick out for easy threes.

On defense, look for lots of easy steals with both Payton and Pierce. Stick to Blount if shot-blocking's your thing. Everyone has clear defensive strengths and weaknesses, so it's easy to know what to do with each man.

DEFEATING

The Celtics are a sweet-shooting team with solid D. Don't noodle around with the ball too much, because these guys can steal the ball. Pound it inside to exploit the relative lack of shot-blocking, especially if you get a matchup with anyone but Blount.

On the defensive side, stay close to Pierce and Payton to prevent long-range gunnery. Go for steals if Blount has the ball. If you have a shot-blocker, goaltend like mad to prevent getting picked apart.

NBA STREET V3

CHARLOTTE BOBCATS

PLAYERS

NAME	NUMBER	SHOTS	DUNKS	BOARDS	POWER	BLOCKS	STEALS	HANDLES	QUICKS	GRAND TOTAL
EMEKA OKAFOR	50	80	85	75	80	70	45	55	65	607
GERALD WALLACE	3	60	90	70	65	45	45	70	80	529
JASON KAPONO	24	80	60	55	40	10	40	75	75	462
PRIMOZ BREZEC	7	65	70	75	60	40	25	40	50	435
BREVIN KNIGHT	22	47	0	25	35	2	74	90	90	386

Emeka Okafor

Emeka Okafor is the Bobcats' first franchise player and a must-play guy if you pick this team. He has a rare combination of high-octane offense (sweet shots, wicked dunks, great power) and great defense (excellent boarding, extremely good blocks).

SUGGESTED LINEUP

- Emeka Okafor (all-around star)
- Gerald Wallace (offense)
- Jason Kapono (shooting, handles)

Gerald Wallace

This fast, high-flying dunkmeister can do a little of everything. Attack the rack whenever you've got him.

Jason Kapono

This Jason Kapono is an offensive-minded player with sweet shots and handles. Get him the rock on offense, and try to play solid position D.

Primoz Brezec

This Slovenian baller possesses good power and dunks. Try to anticipate the opponent's moves, to compensate for his sluggish foot speed.

Brevin Knight

Brevin Knight is a true pass-first point guard. He's got mad handles and speed; if you pick him, be sure to go *nuts* with tricks. Look for alley-oops and trick passes rather than shots. And dunks? Ain't gonna happen.

BEING

As an expansion team, the Bobcats aren't deep. Okafor is rock-solid and Wallace is an explosive dunker, but the drop-off after that is steep. Exploit Okafor's and Wallace's ability to throw down the toughest dunks to compensate for middling handles. If the opponent starts packing the lane too tightly, kick it out to Kapono and let him bomb away.

Defense is a weak spot, save for Okafor's blocks, but there's no help for it. Play position defense and substitute Knight for Kapono if you get desperate for steals.

DEFEATING

The Bobcats' defense is super-porous, unless they take Brevin Knight—in which case their offense is weakened. Go crazy with trick combos and wicked dunks. Fancy moves are easy to execute on this crew.

Okafor is the only shot-blocker, so attack the others and keep track of where Okafor is at all times. He's the guy you don't want to challenge. If Knight's in the game, play the others close, but sag far off of him, daring him to shoot.

CHICAGO BULLS

PLAYERS

NAME	NUMBER	SHOTS	DUNKS	BOARDS	POWER	BLOCKS	STEALS	HANDLES	QUICKS	GRAND TOTAL
TYSON CHANDLER	3	70	75	70	70	60	30	40	65	484
EDDY CURRY	2	65	65	80	80	60	30	40	50	475
KIRK HINRICH	12	80	30	35	25	25	65	80	75	428
ANTONIO DAVIS	34	50	60	75	85	70	35	45	55	511
BEN GORDON	7	80	55	55	50	10	65	80	85	489

Tyson Chandler

Tyson Chandler is a long, tall player who combines powerful dunks with the ability to board and block. Not a bad combination, don't you think? We recommend playing him in every Bulls lineup.

SUGGESTED LINEUP

- Tyson Chandler (dunks, boards, blocks)
- Eddy Curry (dunks, boards, blocks)
- Ben Gordon (shot, handles, steals)

Eddy Curry

Eddy Curry's offensive skills aren't quite as polished as Chandler's, but he's a big, powerful guy, and he, too, can block shots. He's a load in the lane, capable of bowling over opponents on either side of the court.

Throw him in there with Chandler and you've got a hard-dunking team that can swat away shots.

Kirk Hinrich

Kirk Hinrich is a young sharp-shooter with great ball skills. He's also capable of getting steals.

Antonio Davis

This burly, veteran defensive specialist can board, dunk, and knock an opponent on his butt. But with Chandler and Curry in the game, his skills become redundant.

Ben Gordon

Ben Gordon usually edges out Kirk Hinrich in our guard slot. He's just as good as Hinrich with the shots and tricks, and his overall offensive game (read dunks) is a bit more complete.

BEING

This is a potent defensive team, so play it up. Use Chandler and Curry to reject shots, grab boards, and generally terrorize the opposition. Steal the ball and harass the perimeter with Gordon.

Just don't get too fancy with those two on the offensive end; Chandler and Curry can dunk well, but their handles are middling, so stick to the lower-level tricks. Invest your turbo in dunks instead of tricks. If the lane gets crowded, don't forget to look for Gordon on the perimeter.

DEFEATING

The Bulls have two good shot-blockers, so be careful. Do tricks away from the basket and try to lure them out, then nail them with the long-range bomb. Or, give it to your best dunker and challenge the blockers with strong moves—the blockers are good, but not dominant. Emphasize tricky offense; the Bulls will have a hard time keeping up in a high-powered offensive game.

On defense, try to exploit the big guys' lack of handles by stealing at every opportunity. Play up close on Ben Gordon to shut down his outside shot.

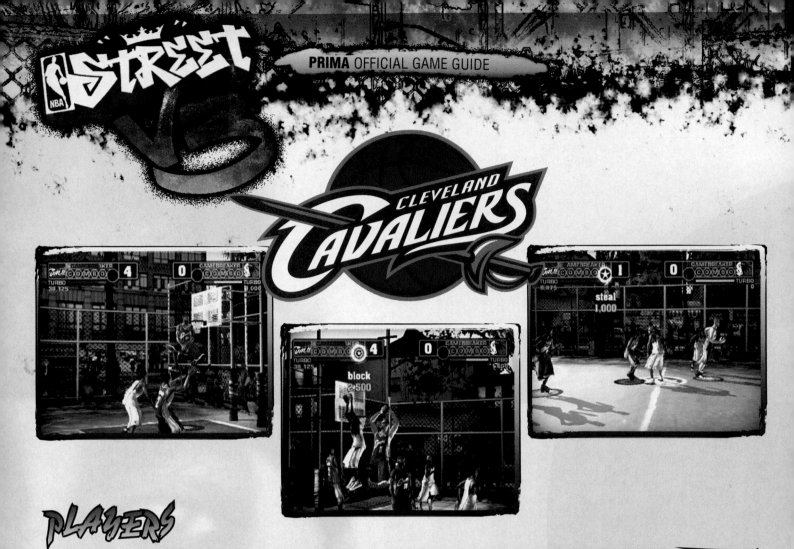

PLAYERS

NAME	NUMBER	SHOTS	DUNKS	BOARDS	POWER	BLOCKS	STEALS	HANDLES	QUICKS	GRAND TOTAL
LEBRON JAMES	23	70	99	65	75	41	61	81	85	601
DAJUAN WAGNER	2	85	41	25	40	21	81	90	90	476
DREW GOODEN	90	70	90	80	55	45	25	40	75	573
ZYDRUNAS ILGAUSKAS	11	70	75	60	60	80	25	30	45	459
JEFF MCINNIS	0	71	30	21	40	21	55	80	75	393

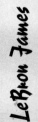

The Cavaliers have this little-known guy called LeBron James. You've probably never heard of him, but he's actually not that bad.

On a more serious note: LeBron is one of the very best players in this game. His dunking skill is tops (only a couple of legends are equal, and *nobody* is better), he's fast, and he can handle all day. He can get steals and can even block some shots. The only reason not to take him is if you're playing a newbie and being nice.

SUGGESTED LINEUP

- LeBron James (duh!)
- Dajuan Wagner (handles, steals, shot)
- Zydrunas Ilgauskas (blocks)

Dajuan Wagner

Dajuan Wagner is a fast, sweet-shooting guard with mad handles and a penchant for larceny. He's an excellent pick. If you select him, make sure he handles as much as possible (and performs lots of top-tier tricks).

Drew Gooden

Drew Gooden is another prime-time dunker, plus he can shoot and board. The only drawback: he's not a great blocker.

Zydrunas Ilgauskas

He's slow as molasses, but you'll probably want to play Ilgauskas anyway, for one simple reason: he's a premier shot-blocker, and there aren't many of those. He's also surprisingly good on offense.

Jeff McInnis

Jeff McInnis is a good shooter and ball handler, but you won't find room for him in most of your lineups. That's because Dajuan Wagner is equal or better in every statistical category.

BEING

The Cavaliers can put three top-notch players on the floor. Use LeBron for fancy moves and thunderous dunks whenever possible; if the opponent gangs up on him, pitch it to Wagner for some fancy tricks and sweet shots. If Ilgauskas is forced to score, skip the tricky dribbles and go straight in for a rumbling dunk.

On defense, use Wagner to harass the perimeter and get steals. Ilgauskas is slow but a monster blocker, which makes him an ideal candidate to sit down low and goaltend. James can get some steals and blocks, but is better at steals—so swipe away when the opponent gets close.

DEFEATING

Don't dribble too much around Wagner, and don't hoist up long shots if Ilgauskas is goaltending. Pass the ball quickly around the perimeter, looking for openings. Strike quickly when you see one, and be prepared to pass or switch to a layup if Ilgauskas is there to stuff you.

On defense, try to slow James down. Play off him a bit more than usual, conceding the jump shot (he's a good shooter, but letting him shoot is better than letting him dunk). You need to block his lane to the basket, because once he takes off you're in trouble.

PLAYERS

NAME	NUMBER	SHOTS	DUNKS	BOARDS	POWER	BLOCKS	STEALS	HANDLES	QUICKS	GRAND TOTAL
MICHAEL FINLEY	4	85	80	40	70	21	70	75	85	532
DIRK NOWITZKI	41	81	60	70	60	50	55	65	70	553
JASON TERRY	31	81	21	45	30	21	75	75	85	465
JERRY STACKHOUSE	42	81	85	40	60	21	50	70	75	524
MARQUIS DANIELS	6	70	70	40	40	40	75	75	75	492

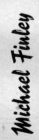

Michael Finley

An All-Star caliber talent, Finley should be on the floor if you play the Mavericks. In addition to a very complete offensive game, he's quite talented at swiping the ball.

SUGGESTED LINEUP

- Michael Finley (all-around game)
- Dirk Nowitzki (all-around game)
- Marquis Daniels (all-around game)

Dirk Nowitzki

Another All-Star, the German sensation is good at just about everything. On offense, he can shoot and dunk. On defense, both his stealing and blocking ability are respectable (an unusual combination). He's another guy you should have in the game at all times.

Jason Terry

Jason Terry is a diminutive, energetic guard with great shooting and speed. Defensively, he can steal the rock with impunity.

Jerry Stackhouse

Stackhouse brings a lot of the same good qualities to the table as Finley. If you're looking for a potent offensive team, he's a good choice for a third man.

Marquis Daniels

Marquis Daniels has a very nice all-around game and complements Finley and Nowitzki well on the court. He can get a few blocks to go with his steals, and his offensive repertoire is big enough to make him a genuine threat.

BEING

This is a team that can do a lot of things well. Finley should do a lot of the heavy lifting on offense, but Nowitzki and Stackhouse (if you play him) are excellent as well. Don't try the very highest-tier tricks, as nobody has out-of-this-world handles.

Everyone on this team can steal, so focus on perimeter defense. Goaltending is a weak strategy because there's not much blocking; get up on your man and try to disrupt the opponent's flow.

DEFEATING

The Mavericks have firepower, but they've also got a hole in the middle. Protect the ball, punch it inside, and go up strong; you usually don't have to worry about getting rejected. Long-range bombs are a good strategy if they leave you open, because you won't have to deal with much goaltending.

On defense, just be solid and contest everything. All of the Mavericks are good offensively, so you can't key on just one guy.

DENVER NUGGETS

PLAYERS

NAME	NUMBER	SHOTS	DUNKS	BOARDS	POWER	BLOCKS	STEALS	HANDLES	QUICKS	GRAND TOTAL
CARMELO ANTHONY	15	81	80	80	65	41	61	81	80	584
ANDRE MILLER	24	75	30	30	55	21	81	85	80	483
MARCUS CAMBY	23	50	80	80	55	85	50	45	70	541
KENYON MARTIN	6	50	80	80	70	80	35	55	70	527
NENÊ	31	70	75	70	70	85	25	50	60	538

Carmelo Anthony

'Melo should be the first guy in your lineup. He's a perfectly complete offensive player, capable of hitting any shot, pulling off any trick, and finishing any dunk. He's also a capable defender; in short, he's the real deal.

SUGGESTED LINEUP

- Cármelo Anthony (complete offensive game)
- Marcus Camby (defense, dunks)
- Nenê (blocks)

Andre Miller

A sweet operator with the rock and a deadly thief without it, Andre Miller is a great point guard. He can chip in with solid offense, to boot.

Marcus Camby

Marcus Camby is a great shot-blocker and dunker, two commodities that are always in demand. He grabs mad boards, too, and can even contribute the occasional steal.

Kenyon Martin

Kenyon Martin possesses a lot of the same skills as Camby, with a few differences. Kenyon is more solid and powerful, while Marcus is leaner and a somewhat better defender.

Kenyon would be a no-brainer to start on most teams, but this one is crowded with big men, so you'll have to make a tough decision.

Nenê

Yet another big guy with talent, the man with one name is another excellent shot-blocker on a team that's blessed with them. His shot is a little purer than that of the other big guys on this team.

BEING

First of all, this is a deep team, so there are lots of great lineups. Our suggested lineup simply reflects our love of shot-blocking. Marcus Camby, Nenê, and Kenyon Martin all have similar abilities and can be swapped at will—and if you want another player who's great with the rock, Andre Miller is a great choice as well. Our point is, you really can't go wrong.

Take advantage of this team's great shot-blockers; goaltend and crowd the paint. Play off your opponents, forcing them into shots instead of dunks. On offense, use Carmelo as much as possible. The big guys are great dunkers but okay handlers, so lay off the very best tricks and go for thunderous dunks.

DEFEATING

If the Nuggets go big (without Andre Miller), you'll face tons of blocking but not much of a steal threat. Trick it up on the perimeter, stringing together wicked chains of fancy moves and going for Gamebreakers early and often. Avoid long-range shots if the Nuggets start goaltending, as you'll get rejected more often than not.

On defense, try to deny 'Melo the ball. Frantically swipe at the ball whenever the bigs get it; they're good dunkers but not extraordinary handlers.

PISTONS
DETROIT

PLAYERS

NAME	NUMBER	SHOTS	DUNKS	BOARDS	POWER	BLOCKS	STEALS	HANDLES	QUICKS	GRAND TOTAL
RICHARD HAMILTON	32	75	65	30	25	30	60	75	75	467
RASHEED WALLACE	36	75	75	75	75	85	50	50	75	596
BEN WALLACE	3	50	81	85	86	90	43	30	60	530
CHAUNCEY BILLUPS	1	71	50	21	55	21	65	85	90	460
TAYSHAUN PRINCE	22	71	80	65	65	40	40	55	70	511

Richard Hamilton

The Man in the Plastic Mask is competent in every facet of the game, but particularly on offense. He's a proven player on a championship team and you can't go wrong with him.

SUGGESTED LINEUP

- Ben Wallace (blocks, dunks)
- Rasheed Wallace (blocks, offense)
- Tayshaun Prince (complete game)

Rasheed Wallace

'Sheed is a premium baller, capable of causing problems for your opponent on both ends of the court. He's one of the few players in the league who can block shots with the best of them, and he combines that ability with a complete (dare I say deadly?) offensive game. He should always be in your lineup.

Ben Wallace

Ben Wallace teaches us that we should, indeed, fear the 'fro. He's the *crème de la crème* shot-blocker, a swatter *par excellence*, and a lot of other cool French stuff as well. Add to that his insane power and monstrous dunks, and you have an unstoppable load. Don't bother with the fancy dribbles. Go straight to the hoop and mash it down!

Chauncey Billups

Chauncey Billups is a big, smart point guard with big handles and speed. He's also a legitimate threat to swipe the ball.

Tayshaun Prince

Possessing a deceptively complete game and Gumby-like flexibility, Tayshaun can do a little bit of everything for your team. He's easy to overlook amidst all the other personalities on the Pistons, but we favor him in our lineups.

BEING

The Wallaces should always be in the game; the third guy is up to you. We take Tayshaun for his big dunks and a smidgen of blocking ability.

If you take this lineup, your strategy is clear-cut. Do tricks in moderation, and finish with the biggest, nastiest dunks you possibly can. Avoid shots whenever possible, as this team lacks pure shooters. Goaltend whenever possible, and look to block shots at the point rather than always going for steals. Blocks, blocks, blocks.

DEFEATING

Even more than usual, you need to set picks, swing the ball, and do everything you can to get a clear lane to the basket. Flying in at a player who's got position will not get it done; you'll get knocked down, or get the ball right back in your face. Go crazy with tricks on the perimeter, exploiting the Pistons' lack of steal ability, and then get the ball in the hole any way you can.

On defense, look for steals, since the Pistons don't have extraordinary ballhandling. You'll need to play solid position defense to cut down on monster dunks. (Stay back a little to encourage shots rather than dunks.)

PLAYERS

NAME	NUMBER	SHOTS	DUNKS	BOARDS	POWER	BLOCKS	STEALS	HANDLES	QUICKS	GRAND TOTAL
JASON RICHARDSON	23	71	90	30	60	45	50	65	70	505
MIKE DUNLEAVY	34	71	55	65	55	35	35	61	60	474
TROY MURPHY	1	71	60	65	50	25	25	40	50	390
CLIFFORD ROBINSON	3	70	60	50	65	45	50	60	65	470
DEREK FISHER	4	80	60	30	50	21	65	85	80	475

Jason Richardson

Jason Richardson brings high-flying dunks and good all-around defense to the table. He's a solid player and the team's best finisher at the hoop.

SUGGESTED LINEUP

- Derek Fisher (handles, steals, shots)
- Jason Richardson (dunks, defense)
- Clifford Robinson (complete game)

Mike Dunleavy

Mike Dunleavy has a nice shot, great smarts, and a decent all-around game.

Troy Murphy

Troy Murphy can shoot, dunk, and board. He's another general-purpose player.

Clifford Robinson

At the risk of sounding like a broken record, this wiry veteran has (dare I say it?) a good all-around game.

Derek Fisher

The former Laker is known for deadly, game-winning shots. He's got classic point guard skills, a great touch, and he can even throw down a tasty dunk or three.

BEING

You've got your work cut out for you with this team. Flow as much low-post offense as possible through Jason Richardson. Use Fisher to launch a barrage of long-range bombs.

On defense, you have no standout performers. Play standard position defense, concentrating on fundamentals (stay in front of your man, contest shots, try to disrupt the fancier tricks).

DEFEATING

When playing the Warriors, turn the game into a carnival of offense. Any strategy will work just fine, as you don't have to worry much about steals or blocks. Defensively, play up on Fisher to prevent those long-range jumpers.

HOUSTON ROCKETS

PLAYERS

NAME	NUMBER	SHOTS	DUNKS	BOARDS	POWER	BLOCKS	STEALS	HANDLES	QUICKS	GRAND TOTAL
TRACY MCGRADY	1	80	90	75	75	60	80	80	85	626
YAO MING	11	51	75	75	75	90	21	35	55	491
JUWAN HOWARD	5	70	65	65	70	35	35	60	65	473
JIM JACKSON	21	85	65	75	75	25	45	65	65	523
MAURICE TAYLOR	2	64	70	65	72	20	37	60	67	460

Tracy McGrady

T-Mac is a phenomenal talent and a big reason the Rockets are so tough. He's been one of the top three offensive players in the league for several years running, and it's easy to see why: No trick or dunk is too tough for him. His defense is exemplary, too, making him a rare complete player. There's no question that he must be on the floor at all times, unless you want to give yourself a handicap.

SUGGESTED LINEUP

- Tracy McGrady (all-around game)
- Yao Ming (blocks, dunks)
- Jim Jackson (shooting, handles)

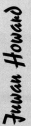

This freakishly skilled Chinese behemoth is one of the best shot-blockers in the game. The fact that he can throw down a nasty dunk is just gravy; you'd put him on the floor for the blocks alone, even if he couldn't find the rim with a telescope. He's another must-play guy.

The veteran forward, one of Michigan's vaunted "Fab Five" in his college days, is a force on offense. This makes him a suitable complement to McGrady.

Jim Jackson is a sweet-shooting veteran guard who works well in any lineup. Outside of McGrady, he's the team's best ball handler.

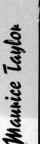

Another Michigan alumnus, Maurice Taylor is yet another all-around solid offensive player.

BEING

Flow your offense through T-Mac as much as possible. He can do it all, so you have lots of freedom when he's got the rock. Stick to straightforward dunks if Yao has the ball; look for the long bomb with Jackson.

On D, prowl the paint with Yao and reject everything in sight. If he goaltends, he can effectively destroy the long game, and drift out to challenge dunks as well. Use T-Mac to harass the perimeter and get steals.

DEFEATING

If Yao is goaltending down low, you'll need to fake him out with smooth tricks. Barreling in for a straight-on power dunk will *not* get the job done. Swing the ball away from McGrady, or risk getting your pocket picked.

On D, try to make anyone but McGrady take the shot. Play position defense and try to block McGrady's lanes; getting too close and too aggressive is a recipe for major schooling. If they feed the ball to Yao down low, try to rip it away before he can throw down the dunk. No plan is foolproof, as this is a great team.

Pacers

PLAYERS

NAME	NUMBER	SHOTS	DUNKS	BOARDS	POWER	BLOCKS	STEALS	HANDLES	QUICKS	GRAND TOTAL
JERMAINE O'NEAL	7	70	90	80	70	81	40	45	70	554
REGGIE MILLER	31	90	41	35	45	21	45	70	75	453
RON ARTEST	91	55	55	85	70	35	85	55	70	602
STEPHEN JACKSON	1	80	75	50	40	50	65	70	70	501
JAMAAL TINSLEY	11	71	25	25	40	21	55	85	75	410

Jermaine O'Neal

This young, All-Star center is a top-flight dunker and a premier shot-blocker. He grabs mad boards, too, and can even get away with a few steals. Must you play him? Yes, you must.

SUGGESTED LINEUP

- Jermaine O'Neal (dunks, blocks)
- Stephen Jackson (all-around game)
- Jamaal Tinsley (handles)

Reggie Miller

Reggie is nearing the end of his career, but he still has one of the sweetest strokes in basketball. If you like the long ball, Reggie is absolutely your man.

Ron Artest

Ron Artest has a freakishly high steal rating for such a big, strong guy. He can put the ball in the hole, but treat him more as a defensive specialist. When he's defending a big guy down low, go for the steal rather than the block.

Stephen Jackson

Stephen Jackson has a very smooth, accomplished all-around game. He really can do a bit of everything, so it's hard to go wrong with him in the lineup.

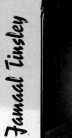

Jamaal Tinsley

Tinsley brings more handles to the table than any other Pacer, so if the funkiest tricks are your thing, you must have him on the floor.

BEING

Tough choices face the Pacers lineup. Artest is a wildly talented defender, but you sacrifice lots of offense with him on the floor. Miller is a lights-out shooter and good with the rock, but the defense and dunks just aren't there.

Your strategy depends on your lineup, but the common threads are these: control O'Neal as much as possible, dunking like crazy on offense (lay off the tricks though) and swatting like crazy on defense. Your choice of second and third players will determine your strategy (long-range gunnery with Miller, wild tricks with Tinsley).

DEFEATING

Play off O'Neal and try to take away his lane; play up on Jackson and Tinsley. Both of them have good shots, so you can take your chances if they put the ball on the floor.

Don't hoist shots unless O'Neal is away from the action and out of goaltending position. Use funky moves to fake him out if he's blocking your path to the hoop. The others aren't great defenders, so swing the ball and try to isolate one of them instead.

LOS ANGELES CLIPPERS

PLAYERS

NAME	NUMBER	SHOTS	DUNKS	BOARDS	POWER	BLOCKS	STEALS	HANDLES	QUICKS	GRAND TOTAL
ELTON BRAND	42	70	75	81	80	80	30	40	70	571
COREY MAGGETTE	50	55	85	60	55	21	45	65	80	516
KERRY KITTLES	30	81	60	30	50	21	45	65	75	459
MARKO JARIC	20	71	40	45	45	25	70	70	70	459
CHRIS WILCOX	54	64	90	75	75	21	21	55	70	526

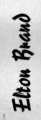

Elton Brand

Elton Brand is the Clippers' go-to guy. He's strong, a great blocker, and offensively complete. He should be in every Clippers lineup.

SUGGESTED LINEUP

- Elton Brand (all-around game)
- Marko Jaric (steals, handles)
- Corey Maggette (offense)

Corey Maggette

A talented dunker with average skills in other areas.

Kenny Kittles

This lanky one-time Net is a good shooter and average defender.

Marko Jaric

Marko is good with the rock, a credible shooter, and a very good perimeter defender.

Chris Wilcox

The highest-flying dunker on the Clippers' roster is not a great defender—but his throwdowns can't be ignored.

BEING

The Clippers are another tough team to play. Flow the offense through Brand, and use him to block shots on D. Look for steals with Jaric. String together lots of low-to-intermediate tricks before every shot. Take some chances, and hope that they pay off!

DEFEATING

Lay the offensive pizzazz on thick, racking up trick points; the Clippers probably can't keep up. Stay away from Brand when you're on offense, and try to block his lanes on defense.

The Clips don't have anyone who can consistently do super-high-level tricks, so they'll probably noodle around with the ball a lot in an attempt to rack up points. Don't allow it! Be aggressive on the perimeter and try for lots of trick counters.

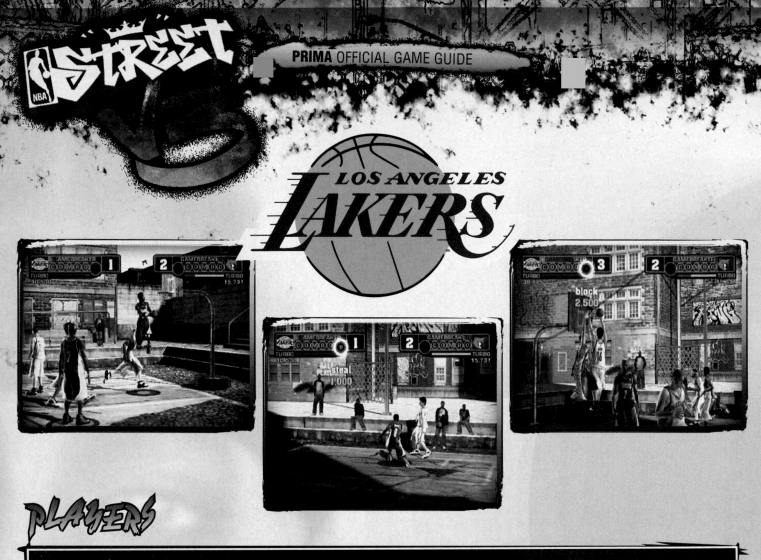

LOS ANGELES LAKERS

PLAYERS

NAME	NUMBER	SHOTS	DUNKS	BOARDS	POWER	BLOCKS	STEALS	HANDLES	QUICKS	GRAND TOTAL
KOBE BRYANT	8	85	90	40	55	45	90	90	90	595
LAMAR ODOM	5	75	75	65	55	70	61	80	80	569
CARON BUTLER	1	80	90	55	65	50	40	50	75	507
BRIAN GRANT	55	65	65	80	85	50	50	45	60	556
VLADE DIVAC	12	70	70	80	90	50	45	50	65	532

Kobe Bryant

Now, who on the Lakers should you put in your lineup? I wonder. How about… hmm…(wait for it)…Kobe Bryant? Yeah, that might be a good choice.

Kobe can do it all on offense. The toughest dunks and tricks are easy for him, and his shot is pure. He's extremely larcenous on D and fast enough to keep up with anybody. Obviously, he goes in every Lakers lineup, always.

SUGGESTED LINEUP

- Kobe Bryant (all-around game)
- Lamar Odom (blocks, handles, offense)
- Vlade Divac (all-around game)

 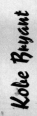

Lamar Odom

About the *only* thing Kobe doesn't excel at is shot-blocking, and that's where Lamar Odom comes in. A very good dunker who's shockingly good at handling the rock (especially considering his size), Odom is a complete offensive player with a great defensive game to boot. Play him.

Caron Butler

Caron Butler is a great offensive player and a good complement to Kobe and Lamar Odom. He's a clear choice for third man if you're gearing up for offense.

Brian Grant

Brian Grant is strong on the boards, and...well, just strong in general. His overall game is solid.

Vlade Divac

Vlade is not the dominant force he once was, but he has extremely good shots for a big man and is capable of taking the ball away with blocks or steals. He's a logical third man if you want a defensive presence.

BEING

Consensus was, the Lakers without Shaq were supposed to be a shell of their former selves. In reality, they're still a very good club. And in a 3-on-3 environment, Kobe's skills take on even more significance.

Flow everything through Kobe, and look to pass if the defense gangs up on him. Kobe can perform the trickiest tricks and fanciest dunks, so you can get loads of trick points with just a few killer moves. Use this advantage to the fullest. Remember that Odom has deceptively good handles too, so he can join in the trick-fest with little fear of getting stripped of the ball.

Use Kobe to snag balls on defense, and play straight-up position D with the big guys. They can both steal and block shots, so you can be as multidimensional as you want.

DEFEATING

The Lakers are hard to handle. Use lots of trick counters to break up the offensive fireworks, as all of their guys can handle. Don't dawdle around Kobe or he'll pick your pocket. Take the ball in strong with your best dunkers, as these guys can block some shots but aren't dominant in that department. Long-range gunnery is also a good option, if used sparingly.

MEMPHIS GRIZZLIES

PLAYERS

NAME	NUMBER	SHOTS	DUNKS	BOARDS	POWER	BLOCKS	STEALS	HANDLES	QUICKS	GRAND TOTAL
PAU GASOL	16	65	60	75	40	75	44	55	65	497
JASON WILLIAMS	2	71	21	21	35	21	75	90	85	421
BONZI WELLS	6	80	50	50	50	21	65	50	75	447
MIKE MILLER	33	81	60	40	35	21	35	65	65	437
JAMES POSEY	41	71	75	45	50	21	55	50	65	475

Pau Gasol

This tall Spanish player is a good blocker and rebounder, and a good offensive player too. Don't get too fancy, and he can get a lot done.

SUGGESTED LINEUP

- Jason Williams (handles, steals)
- Mike Miller (general offense)
- James Posey (dunks)

Jason Williams

Randy Moss' high-school teammate is a wizard with the rock. Load up on fancy tricks on offense, and steal with impunity on D.

Bonzi Wells

Bonzi Wells has a sweet scoring touch and the ability to play perimeter D. His overall game is solid.

Mike Miller

Mike Miller is primarily a shooter, with some handling skills and dunking thrown in for good measure.

James Posey

James Posey's game is competent and well-rounded, with no standout highs or lows.

BEING

The Grizzlies are tough to play because they lack do-everything players. Jason Williams can handle with the best of them, but his finishing ability is not exceptional. You can put Pau Gasol in the lineup for blocking—maybe a good idea—but if you pull Mike Miller to do it, you lose shooting and handles.

Try to pull lots of funky stunts on the perimeter, meanwhile looking for easy alley-oops or gaping holes in the D. On defense, use Gasol to goaltend (if you're playing him) and Williams to steal the rock.

DEFEATING

Aggressively counter tricks on the perimeter, and stay up on your man with in-your-face D. Dare the Grizz to take the ball to the rack. They lack top-flight dunkers, so you don't want to let them hang back and pile up trick points with fancy dribbling.

On offense, just run your standard game plan. Gasol can block some shots and Williams can steal, but overall, you aren't facing exceptional defenders.

STREET V3

MIAMI HEAT

PLAYERS

NAME	NUMBER	SHOTS	DUNKS	BOARDS	POWER	BLOCKS	STEALS	HANDLES	QUICKS	GRAND TOTAL
SHAQUILLE O'NEAL	32	50	81	81	90	81	21	21	30	490
EDDIE JONES	6	80	70	25	55	30	85	75	80	508
DWYANE WADE	3	80	75	75	50	50	75	85	85	579
UDONIS HASLEM	40	51	70	65	55	31	35	45	55	450
WESLEY PERSON	7	81	35	30	30	35	45	55	65	386

Shaquille O'Neal

Here's a guy you might just recognize. And just as you'd expect, he's pretty dominant. His incredible power rating combined with excellent dunk rating gives him total air superiority over lesser defenders. It's hard to block a dunk when you're lying on your back.

Shaq can also swat shots and muscle out players that are trying to penetrate the lane.

Obviously, Shaq needs to play whenever you select the Heat.

SUGGESTED LINEUP

- 🏀 Shaquille O'Neal (power, blocks, dunks)
- 🏀 Eddie Jones (offense, steals)
- 🏀 Dwyane Wade (all-around game)

Eddie Jones

Eddie Jones is a high-octane scorer and a master of the steal. Avoid the very top-tier dunks and tricks with him, but feel free to do all the others.

Dwyane Wade

Dwyane Wade is another top-notch scorer with solid defense. Combined with Shaq and Eddie Jones, the result is a very hard team to beat.

Udonis Haslem

Haslem is a good dunker with decent all-around skills.

Wesley Person

This veteran three-point specialist, once known as a world-class trash talker, still has a sweet shot.

BEING

One nice thing about the Heat: there's only one prime-time lineup, so you don't need to agonize over who to put in the game.

This is a fun, easy team to play. All three guys can flat-out play offense, though there are a few differences. Dunk exclusively with Shaq; don't shoot. Do the highest-tier tricks with Wade, but nobody else. And on defense, make sure to control Shaq if you want to pursue a goaltending strategy. The two perimeter guys can both steal, which makes your job extremely easy.

DEFEATING

The Heat are an extremely tough team this year, so no matter your strategy, you're in for a wild ride.

On offense, keep the ball moving to avoid steals. Take quick shots and dunks, because if you take your time and allow Shaq to get in your way, you've got problems. Use picks and look to shoot the long ball if you can. Try to manufacture situations where you're driving to the hoop against anyone but Shaq.

On defense, try to steal the ball anytime Shaq gets it. Play off Jones and Wade a bit, taking away the easy lanes to the basket.

MILWAUKEE
BUCKS

PLAYERS

NAME	NUMBER	SHOTS	DUNKS	BOARDS	POWER	BLOCKS	STEALS	HANDLES	QUICKS	GRAND TOTAL
MICHAEL REDD	22	81	70	65	50	11	65	80	80	524
DESMOND MASON	24	65	90	55	40	31	55	60	70	490
KEITH VAN HORN	44	75	75	65	55	35	55	65	75	547
T.J. FORD	11	65	35	40	21	11	65	90	90	430
JOE SMITH	8	65	70	70	70	45	35	50	65	481

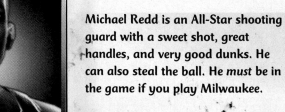

Michael Redd is an All-Star shooting guard with a sweet shot, great handles, and very good dunks. He can also steal the ball. He *must* be in the game if you play Milwaukee.

SUGGESTED LINEUP

- Michael Redd (offense, steals)
- Desmond Mason (dunks)
- T.J. Ford (handles)

Desmond Mason

The "Cowboy" is known for his high-flying dunks. Look to attack the rim at all times if he's in your lineup.

Keith Van Horn

Keith Van Horn has a very complete game, with an emphasis on offense.

T.J. Ford

T.J. Ford is a prototypical pass-first point guard, with blazing speed and mad handles. He's a great choice if complicated tricks are your thing.

Joe Smith

The former No. 1 draft pick has a nice offensive touch and is a force on the boards.

BEING

The Bucks have no shot-blocking presence, so don't worry about swatting shots. All of the Bucks have reasonable steal skill, so try to purloin the ball at every opportunity. Use trick counters to prevent uncontested romps to the basket.

On offense, flow through Redd as much as possible, dishing to Mason for wicked dunks whenever you get the opportunity. Ford is no scorer, so only have him shoot when he's wide open.

DEFEATING

Pick apart the Bucks' interior, and capitalize on their lack of shot-blocking. Hammer the ball inside with high-level dunkers and throw it down. If you have a great shooter, feel free to jack up long-range shots, as the Bucks can't effectively goaltend.

Smother Redd on the defensive end, and dare Ford to shoot the ball.

MINNESOTA
TIMBERWOLVES

PLAYERS

NAME	NUMBER	SHOTS	DUNKS	BOARDS	POWER	BLOCKS	STEALS	HANDLES	QUICKS	GRAND TOTAL
KEVIN GARNETT	21	70	90	85	80	70	60	65	85	627
SAM CASSELL	19	75	21	21	45	21	75	85	80	442
LATRELL SPREWELL	8	80	90	25	70	21	70	80	85	529
WALLY SZCZERBIAK	10	81	60	41	65	21	50	60	65	456
TROY HUDSON	16	60	0	35	50	21	45	81	70	379

Kevin Garnett

The Kid is undeniably one of the finest players in the league. His powerful dunks are his best offensive weapon, but he can shoot it, too. He's a complete player on D, capable of taking the ball away, blocking shots, or knocking down weaker opponents in mid-air jousts. No question, Garnett is an extraordinary player and must be in your lineup at all times.

SUGGESTED LINEUP

- Kevin Garnett (duh!)
- Latrell Sprewell (complete game)
- Sam Cassell (handles, steals)

Sam Cassell

The veteran point guard (and newly minted All-Star) has a nice shot and mad handles. He's also an excellent perimeter defender.

Latrell Sprewell

Spree brings an absolutely complete offensive game and excellent defense to the table. He's a must-play guy to go along with Garnett.

BE7UG

Use Garnett for monstrous, impossible-to-contest dunks, but flow much of the offense through Sprewell, who's an excellent shooter and handler. Flip it to Cassell to execute the funkiest of tricks.

On defense, look for steals. Garnett is a good shot-blocker but he can steal as well, so don't get too focused on swats. Learn to use his versatility, using whatever move the situation calls for.

Wally Szczerbiak

Wally has a sweet shot and polished offensive game. He's known for hitting clutch shots and bringing serious attitude to the floor.

DEFEAT7UG

Swing the ball to open lanes, and finish with quick dunks. Don't hold the ball too long, or the Wolves will steal it. If they play loose D, keep doing tricks until they get up in your face.

On defense, you won't get many steals from these guys. Focus on trick counters with your best theft artist, and force outside shots if at all possible.

Troy Hudson

This diminutive point guard can handle the rock with skill. But with Cassell on the roster, it'll be hard to get him any playing time.

PLAYERS

NAME	NUMBER	SHOTS	DUNKS	BOARDS	POWER	BLOCKS	STEALS	HANDLES	QUICKS	GRAND TOTAL
JASON KIDD	5	71	45	60	60	21	85	90	85	524
VINCE CARTER	15	80	90	45	65	70	55	81	80	581
RICHARD JEFFERSON	24	51	90	35	70	35	45	70	70	490
JASON COLLINS	35	65	65	75	75	55	30	45	50	498
RON MERCER	1	75	75	30	50	21	45	65	75	437

Jason Kidd

This many-time All-Star is noted for his excellent court vision. He's a wizard with the rock and a great defender. He should always be in your lineup.

SUGGESTED LINEUP

- Jason Kidd (handles, steals)
- Vince Carter (complete game)
- Richard Jefferson (dunks, handles)

Vince Carter

"Vinsanity" is an offensive machine. He's best known for his aerial acrobatics, but he's one of the few complete offensive players that can do any dunk or trick, and shoot the rock as well. Throw in the ability to swat shots, and you've got the definition of a go-to guy.

Richard Jefferson

A talented handler and dunkmeister extraordinaire, Jefferson's role is to give your offensive game a kick in the pants.

Jason Collins

Jason Collins has a good all-around game. While not renowned for it, he can swat a few shots—in fact, he's easily the team's best shot-blocker.

Ron Mercer

Mercer has a good offensive game, making him a nice choice for run-and-gun lineups.

BEING

The loss of Kenyon Martin rocked the Nets, and left them without a strong interior presence. They got a big boost recently, however, when they traded for explosive scorer Vince Carter. This trade turns the Nets into an instant offensive powerhouse; needless to say, you should let Carter do the heavy lifting when it's time to finish a dunk.

On D, control Kidd as much as possible and practice a bit of thievery.

DEFEATING

The Nets have no big defenders, so charge in and rock the rim.

On defense, play back on Kidd and Jefferson and allow them to shoot it. You won't steal the ball from Kidd very often, but well-timed trick counters with a great defender can prevent the Nets from racking up ridiculous trick points.

NBA STREET V3

NEW ORLEANS HORNETS

PLAYERS

NAME	NUMBER	SHOTS	DUNKS	BOARDS	POWER	BLOCKS	STEALS	HANDLES	QUICKS	GRAND TOTAL
BARON DAVIS	1	80	70	60	50	21	75	85	85	528
JAMAL MASHBURN	24	81	60	55	70	21	70	75	70	526
P.J. BROWN	42	50	65	80	80	50	30	35	70	505
DAVID WESLEY	4	71	10	21	55	21	65	80	75	403
JAMAAL MAGLOIRE	21	55	75	70	75	80	21	30	45	475

Baron Davis

Baron Davis has All-Star handles and shots, and he can play D as well, with a renowned penchant for steals. He's a must-play guy whenever you pick the Hornets.

SUGGESTED LINEUP

- Baron Davis (offense, steals)
- Jamaal Magloire (blocks, dunks)
- Jamal Mashburn (all-around game)

Jamal Mashburn

Mashburn is a complete player, capable of just about anything you ask of him. He's a particularly good shooter and perimeter defender.

P.J. Brown

Praised as a tough player, Brown is a powerful presence and a demon on the boards.

David Wesley

This diminutive speedster, a Hornet from the very start, takes excellent care of the rock. He can hit shots and swipe the occasional ball as well.

Jamaal Magloire

Another physically strong player and must-play guy, Magloire brings crucial shot-blocking ability in addition to his tough dunks. He rounds out a good defensive team.

BEING

This team can shoot the three, so look to generate wide-open looks with picks and aggressive passing. Pound it inside with Magloire to change it up.

On D, send Magloire down low to swat away weak shots. Baron Davis can guard the perimeter effectively. Try to shut down tricks as much as possible, or you'll fall behind in the Gamebreaker department.

DEFEATING

Play up close and take away those long shots. If Magloire gets the ball, immediately look to steal; his handles are very low, and you can often rip the ball away before he makes his move.

On the flip side, don't toss up too much long-range stuff, or Magloire will goaltend it. Balance your offense and move the ball. Immediately attack the rim if Magloire is out of position.

NEW YORK KNICKS

PLAYERS

NAME	NUMBER	SHOTS	DUNKS	BOARDS	POWER	BLOCKS	STEALS	HANDLES	QUICKS	GRAND TOTAL
STEPHON MARBURY	3	80	60	21	55	21	75	90	90	495
ALLAN HOUSTON	20	90	60	40	55	21	65	75	75	503
JAMAL CRAWFORD	11	80	45	45	40	45	75	75	75	491
TIM THOMAS	5	71	80	45	70	25	50	65	65	479
PENNY HARDAWAY	1	71	55	30	60	25	60	80	75	460

Stephon Marbury

Stephon Marbury is the heart of the new-look Knicks. He's got the quicks moves of a true top-shelf point guard, and his shooting is extremely pure. He's also a wicked dunker for his size and a good perimeter defender. In short, he's a must-play guy.

SUGGESTED LINEUP

- Stephon Marbury (complete offense, steals)
- Allan Houston (shooting, steals)
- Jamal Crawford (shooting, steals)

Allan Houston

Allan Houston is more shooter than slammer; in fact, he's one of the premier sharpshooters in the league. His defense isn't bad, either. Look to stroke the long jumper whenever Houston is on the floor.

Jamal Crawford

Jamal Crawford is a lot like Allan Houston. His shot is pure, his perimeter D is good, and he can handle the rock. The bottom line: He's another solid Knicks player.

Tim Thomas

Tim Thomas, formerly of the Bucks, is a valuable addition to the lineup—mainly for his power dunks. He can also shoot and handle, but slamming is his specialty.

Penny Hardaway

Penny's come a long way from his early days in the league, as Shaq's sidekick in Orlando. He's still got top-notch handles and solid man-to-man defensive skills.

BEING

This lineup features three good handlers and no great dunkers, so work the tricks like crazy and finish with shots or simple dunks. (You can sub in Thomas for Crawford to get dunking power, but then you sacrifice defense. You make the call.)

All three players can steal but none can block. Harass the ball carrier down the court and constantly swipe at the ball, because you have little chance of altering a shot once it's in midair. When the shot clock gets low, pack into the lane to discourage monster dunks.

DEFEATING

Pound the ball down low and exploit the Knicks' lack of power and shot-blocking. A strong dunking team will win those mid-air duels. Don't dribble too much, and be crafty with your tricks, as everyone on this team can swipe the ball from a careless player.

Because the Knicks are a sweet-shooting team with a lack of dunking skills, man up close to contest those shots. Use trick counters early and often. Force the Knicks to drive, and then try to swat shots with aggressive defense.

PLAYERS

NAME	NUMBER	SHOTS	DUNKS	BOARDS	POWER	BLOCKS	STEALS	HANDLES	QUICKS	GRAND TOTAL
STEVE FRANCIS	3	75	90	50	55	21	80	90	90	554
GRANT HILL	33	81	70	45	70	30	65	80	80	554
CUTTINO MOBLEY	5	75	55	21	60	21	70	75	75	459
HEDO TURKOGLU	15	80	50	55	55	40	70	70	70	507
DWIGHT HOWARD	12	65	80	70	70	65	21	40	40	465

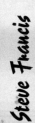

Steve Francis

"Stevie Franchise" is an offensive powerhouse, with special emphasis on slams and handles. He's one of those rare players who can follow up a top-flight trick with a top-flight dunk. His ability to swipe the ball is also exceptional, making his inclusion in your lineups a no-brainer.

SUGGESTED LINEUP

- Steve Francis (all-around game)
- Grant Hill (offense)
- Hedo Turkoglu (shooting, steals, handles)

Grant Hill

It's nice to see Grant Hill back in action after so many injury-riddled seasons. He's in fine form, too, sporting a sweet shot, powerful dunks, and good D. He deserves a place on the floor and not just for sentimental reasons.

Cuttino Mobley

Cuttino Mobley is a "little bit of everything" player, with good offensive skills and the ability to guard opposing small men. He's fast and capable of pulling off all but the trickiest moves.

Hedo Turkoglu

Hedo Turkoglu has hopped teams recently, but that's not because he's a slouch—rather, it's because he's in demand. He's not a great dunker, but his other offensive skills are top-notch—and like many others on this team, the man can steal.

Dwight Howard

The rookie is a dunking powerhouse, suitable for any lineup that emphasizes down-low offense. Also, though he's not a premier shot-blocker, he's the only Orlando player who's competent in that department.

BEING

Steve Francis and Grant Hill are shoo-ins; the third man is up to you. We went with Hedo for his sweet stroke and ability to *occasionally* reject a shot.

Stevie Franchise and Grant Hill are your first options on offense; use them to work the ball around, and take an opening if you see it. Use Hedo as a spot-up shooter to loosen the defense with long bombs.

All three players can pilfer the ball, so swipe constantly and harass the ball carrier down the court. Be particularly aggressive when stealing from the opponent's big guys. Swat at shots, but don't expect much; you need to play most of your D before the ball gets airborne.

DEFEATING

This is another center-less team with good handling and steals, so work the ball inside quickly, and throw down lots of powerful dunks. Shoot the wide-open shot with little fear of goaltending. You'll be very efficient if you don't stand around with the ball.

Defending against this team is difficult, because nobody is careless or unskilled with the ball. Instead of constantly swiping, try a few well-placed trick counters and then settle in for some blocked shots. A strong defender can often knock down incoming Magic players, as well as their shots.

76ERS

PLAYERS

NAME	NUMBER	SHOTS	DUNKS	BOARDS	POWER	BLOCKS	STEALS	HANDLES	QUICKS	GRAND TOTAL
ALLEN IVERSON	3	90	65	25	55	21	90	90	90	529
GLENN ROBINSON	31	81	60	45	70	35	50	60	70	502
KENNY THOMAS	9	75	65	80	70	35	60	55	65	516
CORLISS WILLIAMSON	14	50	60	60	80	21	35	61	50	432
SAMUEL DALEMBERT	1	50	75	60	50	85	35	55	65	479

The 76ers have been Iverson's team for quite awhile now, and there's a good reason why. His size prevents him from being a stellar dunker or shot-blocker, but other aspects of his offensive game are nothing short of spectacular. He shoots lights-out; he can perform mad tricks; his steals are out-of-this-world. He goes in every lineup, every time.

SUGGESTED LINEUP

- Allen Iverson (all-star game)
- Kenny Thomas (boards, steals)
- Samuel Dalembert (blocks)

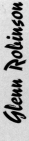

Glenn "Big Dog" Robinson is a shooter first. He can throw down a few dunks as well, but if he's in your lineup you must look to capitalize on his shot.

Kenny Thomas has an eclectic mix of skills—great on the boards, very powerful, but (unfortunately) not a shot-blocker.

Corliss Williamson is another journeyman with solid offensive skills. His physical strength is his most outstanding quality.

You will play Dalembert for his blocking ability. Without him, the team can't swat much of anything; with him, opposing teams need to think twice before putting up shots.

BEING

This lineup is fairly one-dimensional on offense, requiring you to flow through Iverson most of the time. Fortunately, he's talented enough that you can get away with it. Pass to teammates mainly to get Iverson free; then get the ball right back to Iverson and put some nasty moves on the opposition.

Iverson can hawk the ball on defense, and Kenny Thomas can also do so, to a lesser extent. Dalembert should goaltend as much as possible. He's more of a finesse blocker than a power blocker, so stand back near the hoop to avoid getting trampled.

DEFEATING

Dunk with your most powerful player in an attempt to mash Dalembert. Be very careful about dribbles and trick moves around Iverson; you might consider keeping the ball away from his man at all times. If he comes off his man to double up on the guy with the ball, kick it back to the open man for the long jumper.

You probably can't shut down all of Iverson's trick moves, but his middling dunk ability means you can sometimes swat the finishing shot. Goaltend as much as possible to neutralize his long-range shooting.

PHOENIX SUNS

PLAYERS

NAME	NUMBER	SHOTS	DUNKS	BOARDS	POWER	BLOCKS	STEALS	HANDLES	QUICKS	GRAND TOTAL
STEVE NASH	13	81	0	25	50	21	81	85	90	447
SHAWN MARION	31	70	75	90	70	75	80	60	85	637
AMARE STOUDEMIRE	32	65	85	70	75	65	40	50	65	547
JOE JOHNSON	2	71	55	45	40	25	30	60	65	396
QUENTIN RICHARDSON	3	71	65	55	40	45	55	45	75	454

Steve Nash

This former Maverick is just the man you want running the show. He's outstanding at handling and stealing the ball, and he can put up long-range bombs whenever the defense is packing the lane.

SUGGESTED LINEUP

- Steve Nash (handles, steals, shots)
- Shawn Marion (all-around game with defensive focus)
- Amare Stoudemire (dunks, defense)

Shawn Marion

An absolutely complete defensive player and monster rebounder, Marion also has a solid offensive game.

Amare Stoudemire

The lanky Stoudemire is a top-flight power dunker and all-around quality defender.

Joe Johnson

Joe Johnson is either a big guard or a small forward, however you look at it. Regardless, he's a consistent performer.

Quentin Richardson

Quentin Richardson is a good shooter and competent defender.

BEING

Do tricks with Nash, and look to finish them with long-range bombs. Or, pitch it in to Marion and Stoudemire for dunks. You don't have players who can do *both* the highest-tier tricks and dunks, so be mindful of who you've got, and play to their strengths.

Marion is your best overall defender, capable of steals and blocks. Keep him in the paint, and use Nash to harass the opposing guards.

DEFEATING

Crash the lanes, because Phoenix's shot-blocking is good but not great. Beware the steals; there are two very competent thieves on this team. Focus on power dunks over fancy tricks.

Play up on Nash and try to prevent excessive tricks (easier said than done). If he drives the lane, okay; he can't dunk, and you can reject a layup. Play a bit off the other two, as their shots aren't nearly as sweet.

PORTLAND TRAIL BLAZERS

PLAYERS

NAME	NUMBER	SHOTS	DUNKS	BOARDS	POWER	BLOCKS	STEALS	HANDLES	QUICKS	GRAND TOTAL
ZACH RANDOLPH	50	70	75	85	80	60	50	65	65	600
DARIUS MILES	23	60	90	45	41	70	55	51	85	520
DAMON STOUDAMIRE	3	71	0	25	30	21	80	90	90	411
DEREK ANDERSON	1	71	80	30	35	21	75	75	85	475
SHAREEF ABDUR-RAHIM	33	75	80	85	70	30	40	60	70	546

Zach Randolph

Zach Randolph is a strong player with a complete game. Powerful dunks are perhaps his best skill, but he's also a capable shot-blocker, and he's truly good in all facets of the game. A real all-purpose player.

SUGGESTED LINEUP

- Zach Randolph (complete game)
- Darius Miles (blocks, dunks)
- Damon Stoudamire (handles, steals)

Darius Miles

Darius Miles is still just a youngster, but his dunking skill is exceptional. He's also the team's best shot-blocker, making him a force to be reckoned with.

Damon Stoudamire

Mighty Mouse won't win any dunk contests, and his shot is okay but not great. His strengths are his superb ballhandling and perimeter defense. Look to rack up trick points and then dish for the score.

Derek Anderson

Derek is a multifaceted guard who can score, steal, and handle the rock. He's a genuine asset on the floor.

Shareef Abdur-Rahim

Lately of the Hawks, Shareef is a complete scorer. His defensive skills are adequate, but it's his ability to fill up the basket that always turns heads.

BEING

Randolph and Miles are easy picks, but the third man is tricky. Damon Stoudamire is the big-name choice, and his handles and steals are sweet—hence the pick. But his combination of so-so shots and inability to dunk make it too easy to ignore him on defense. You'll have to compensate with mad tricks and creative passing. Ultimately, who you choose depends on your personal playing style.

This lineup features a mix of power, dunking, and handles, but shooting is a sore spot. Fill up the basket with thunderous dunks, and plug the lanes with aggressive low-post defense. Try not to get suckered into taking long shots. Instead, use Stoudamire for tricks and funky passes, then dish it off and bowl over your opponents on the way to the basket.

DEFEATING

If the Blazers play Stoudamire, play up on him as he brings the ball down the court, then fade off of him. Give him some room on D, challenging him to shoot. In fact, give everyone on this team some room; shooting is not a strong point, so your goal is to prevent dunks.

The Blazers' shot-blockers are good but not premium, so take the ball in with your top dunker and you can usually finish.

If your opponent chooses not to use Stoudamire in an attempt to load up on dunking and general-purpose offense, the Blazers will have weak ballhandling. Hawk the ball and go for steals at every opportunity.

PLAYERS

NAME	NUMBER	SHOTS	DUNKS	BOARDS	POWER	BLOCKS	STEALS	HANDLES	QUICKS	GRAND TOTAL
CHRIS WEBBER	4	70	75	90	90	80	50	60	80	600
MIKE BIBBY	10	71	21	21	30	21	80	85	80	422
PEJA STOJAKOVIC	16	90	50	55	65	21	65	65	65	494
BRAD MILLER	52	70	50	80	75	75	60	45	50	560
DOUG CHRISTIE	13	81	65	21	50	30	75	60	70	466

Chris Webber

C-Webb is a very talented scorer, but his true gift in *NBA STREET V3* is rejecting shots. His combination of great blocks and off-the-charts power means he's not just able to swat shots; he can also take on the biggest opponents as they drive the lane, knocking them off course and foiling their plans for easy down-low scoring.

SUGGESTED LINEUP

- Chris Webber (blocks, boards, dunks)
- Peja Stojakovic (shots, handles)
- Brad Miller (blocks, boards)

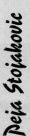

Mike Bibby

Mike Bibby's wizardry with the ball makes him a top-notch handler and perimeter defender. His shot is good as well, but avoid dunks against competent defenders.

Peja Stojakovic

Peja is a shooting specialist, winner of more than one three-point bombing contest. He can play some D and score in other ways, but the long ball is where he really shines.

Brad Miller

Brad Miller brings an unusual mix of power and good shooting touch—and his ability to block shots is welcome indeed. Pair him up with Webber and you've got a team with extra-tough interior defense.

Doug Christie

This lanky scorer has a deft shooting touch and a knack for taking away the ball.

BEING

The Kings have lots of talent, but it's spread around in such a way that there's no clear-cut starting lineup; you have to make sacrifices. The lineup we picked emphasizes blocks and shooting, but lacks top-flight dunk artists and handlers. You can solve the handling problem by putting in Bibby, but only at the cost of blocks and/or shooting touch.

Get the most out of your shot-blockers. Pack the lane; goaltend; challenge every drive. You won't get many steals, but if you hang back a little you can make it tough to put the ball in the hole.

On the offensive end, work it around to free up Peja, and rely on his feathery shooting touch. Webber can power in for solid dunks as well. Miller is more shooter than dunker despite his power, so fire away if he's left open.

DEFEATING

Depending on the chosen lineup, the Kings will have an obvious weakness or two. The suggested lineup is vulnerable to steals, so heavy pressure is recommended. Especially play up on Stojakovic and Miller, whose shots are much more potent than their dunks.

Offense is tough to come by with those shot-blockers in the game, so score quickly on open looks, rather than noodling around and performing excessive tricks. You probably won't bull over these guys in the paint, so if you're forced to face down a defender, use a single potent trick to fake him out of the way.

SAN ANTONIO SPURS

PLAYERS

NAME	NUMBER	SHOTS	DUNKS	BOARDS	POWER	BLOCKS	STEALS	HANDLES	QUICKS	GRAND TOTAL
TIM DUNCAN	21	50	80	85	80	80	41	65	75	580
TONY PARKER	9	75	0	30	40	21	85	90	90	442
MANU GINOBILI	20	80	50	45	45	45	85	80	80	531
BRENT BARRY	17	81	70	30	45	21	60	70	65	461
ROBERT HORRY	5	80	60	55	55	65	60	50	60	490

Tim Duncan

The savvy young center was a leading candidate for last year's MVP award. He's a power dunker who's nearly impossible to deny, a monster on the boards, and a prime-time shot-blocker to boot. He must be on the floor for any Spurs team.

SUGGESTED LINEUP

- Tim Duncan (all-around game)
- Tony Parker (handles, steals)
- Manu Ginobili (handles, steals, shots)

Tony Parker

This streaky French import is truly dynamic with the rock, and a premier on-ball defender. Don't worry about his lack of dunk ability; just put him on the floor and revel in his speed and agility.

Manu Ginobili

Another prime-time ball handler and lights-out shooter, the fiery Argentinean's most outstanding quality is his ability to snatch the ball from the opposition's hands.

Brent Barry

Brent Barry is a powerhouse in all facets of the offensive game and a decent perimeter defender.

Robert Horry

Perhaps best known for hitting monstrous game-winning shots with the Lakers, Horry was a big dunker in his prime. He now relies on a sweet shot and a balanced defensive game.

BEING

This is one talented defensive team. Prowl the lane with Duncan and rack up blocks, or switch to Parker or Ginobili and take advantage of their freakishly high steal ratings. Aggressive defense is your ticket to victory.

On offense, just stay the course. Slam it down low with Duncan for easy points, and look for long-range stuff with Ginobili. Both Parker and Ginobili are dunk-deficient but trick-happy, so pile on the fancy tricks to get easy Gamebreakers.

DEFEATING

Pass frequently and take your shots and dunks when you can; don't shuffle around too much with the ball. Waiting too long on the perimeter results in steals, and slow-developing dunks or shots are often blocked by Duncan. Try to be efficient on offense, and then spend a lot of energy on defense.

Play off Parker as the clock winds down, trying to bait him into shooting. Play up on Duncan, trying for steals—because with his power, you probably aren't going to reject his dunks.

PLAYERS

NAME	NUMBER	SHOTS	DUNKS	BOARDS	POWER	BLOCKS	STEALS	HANDLES	QUICKS	GRAND TOTAL
RAY ALLEN	34	90	70	30	65	21	70	75	80	537
RASHARD LEWIS	7	71	80	60	55	45	60	60	70	508
VLADIMIR RADMANOVIC	77	71	65	65	35	35	25	50	60	484
RONALD MURRAY	22	75	75	45	55	25	25	70	70	462
LUKE RIDNOUR	8	75	21	35	45	15	35	70	75	380

Ray Allen

"Sugar Ray" has one of the game's purest shots, so he's your man if you like to shoot the long J. His other offensive stats are top-flight as well, so you can run a complete offense through him.

SUGGESTED LINEUP

- 🏀 Ray Allen (overall game)
- 🏀 Rashard Lewis (dunks, overall game)
- 🏀 Ronald Murray (offense)

Rashard Lewis

A dunker to complement Ray Allen's shooting, Rashard has good defensive skills and a high level of competence in all areas.

Vladimir Radmanovic

The native of Serbia and Montenegro has a polished offensive game. He's a good contributor on the glass.

Ronald Murray

Ronald Murray is skilled at putting the ball in the hoop. His sweet handles make him a legitimate threat. Despite a lack of defensive presence, we think he's Seattle's best third man.

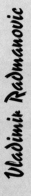

Luke Ridnour

The curly-haired Oregon product shoots first and asks questions later. He's another good ball handler.

BEING

Are you ready to run and gun? You'd better be if you chose the Sonics, as you won't win games with your defense. Fire away with Ray Allen, or throw down big dunks with Rashard Lewis and Ronald Murray. Stick to mid-level tricks all around. Everyone can shoot—not just Ray—so focus on getting guys open on the perimeter. The long game can pay off handsomely.

On defense, play Ray or Rashard and go for steals. You need to pick pockets before the ball gets pounded down low, because nobody has the power or shot-blocking skills to stand up to a monster dunker.

DEFEATING

Do a couple of tricks, then pound the ball inside and punish them. High-power players will romp uncontested through this center-less Seattle team.

On defense, man up extra-close and take away the long bomb. Rely on defense to swat away those not-so-powerful dunks. Don't give up on blocks if you get beat; you can get from-behind blocks on these guys.

PLAYERS

NAME	NUMBER	SHOTS	DUNKS	BOARDS	POWER	BLOCKS	STEALS	HANDLES	QUICKS	GRAND TOTAL
JALEN ROSE	5	80	70	40	65	25	75	81	81	522
DONYELL MARSHALL	42	65	70	75	52	50	50	55	70	532
ERIC WILLIAMS	17	65	65	65	60	21	55	70	65	484
MORRIS PETERSON	24	75	70	40	45	21	40	65	70	452
RAFER ALSTON	11	71	0	40	35	21	75	90	99	443

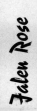

Jalen Rose is another potent offensive force who can shoot and dunk, and pull off any trick in the book.

SUGGESTED LINEUP

- Jalen Rose (complete game)
- Eric Williams (complete game)
- Rafer Alston (handles, speed)

Donyell Marshall

Donyell Marshall is a much-traveled forward with a genuinely balanced skill set. He can do a little of everything, making him a very flexible player.

Eric Williams

Eric Williams's stats are evenly distributed; his best quality is his steadiness with the rock.

Morris Peterson

Mo Pete is a scorer first and foremost. Take advantage of his dunking skills.

Rafer Alston

"Skip" was a playground legend before joining the NBA; his lightning speed and wicked handles make it clear why. He can play good perimeter defense, too.

BEING

You might be surprised at the Raptors' potency, because their recent NBA record has not been stellar. But their emphasis on high-flying offense and wicked tricks makes them ideal for *NBA STREET V3*. Eric and Jalen are easy choices; the third man depends on your preferences. We took Rafer for his mad handles and steals.

This lineup can do any trick at any time. Spread the ball around and pull off high-value tricks at will, and don't worry about getting the ball stolen.

Look for steals with Alston and Rose. This is a good defensive team, so step up and harass the ball carrier.

DEFEATING

The Raptors can steal the ball, so swing-pass around the perimeter rather than dribbling excessively. Because all of the Raptors can pull off spectacular tricks, get ready with the trick counters.

PLAYERS

NAME	NUMBER	SHOTS	DUNKS	BOARDS	POWER	BLOCKS	STEALS	HANDLES	QUICKS	GRAND TOTAL
ANDREI KIRILENKO	47	71	70	70	40	80	75	55	70	581
CARLOS BOOZER	5	75	75	81	81	41	41	60	75	536
MATT HARPRING	15	70	55	45	65	21	45	55	65	439
MEHMET OKUR	13	80	70	55	70	60	40	45	40	474
CARLOS ARROYO	30	70	0	25	25	15	75	85	90	418

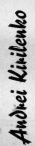

Andrei Kirilenko

The angular Russian is a defensive madman, combining top-tier blocking skills with the ability to steal the rock at any time. Throw in a well-developed offensive game, and you have a top-flight player who's extremely tough to handle.

SUGGESTED LINEUP

- Andrei Kirilenko (all-around game with defensive emphasis)
- Carlos Boozer (offense, power)
- Carlos Arroyo (handles)

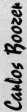

Carlos Boozer

Carlos Boozer plays with ferocity, ripping down boards and throwing down dunks with unquestioned authority. When he rumbles into the lane, not many players have a chance to stop him.

Matt Harpring

A good shooter with intermediate skills, Harpring will have a tough time cracking your lineup.

Mehmet Okur

The burly Turkish import has a compelling mix of powerful dunks and a silky-smooth shot. He can swat shots, too. He's an excellent addition to your roster.

Carlos Arroyo

Arroyo won't dunk on anyone, but he's far and away the best handler on the Utah roster. For that reason alone you'll probably want to play him.

BEING

It kills us not to put Okur in the starting lineup. We'd love to put him in over Arroyo, but without Arroyo the Jazz are dangerously lacking in ball skills. As a result they'd have a tough time with tricks and would be vulnerable to steals. Still, you may want to go with a power lineup and replace Arroyo with Okur; in that case, pass often and beware the steal.

Use Kirilenko to lock down opposing offenses; he's good enough (and multitalented enough) to take on the other team's best player. Exploit Boozer's power on offense, knocking down anyone that gets in his path.

DEFEATING

The Jazz are light on handlers, making them vulnerable to steals (unless Arroyo has the ball) and preventing them from doing high-level tricks (again, unless Arroyo has it). Combo-break frequently against Arroyo, and try to steal against the others. On offense, work the ball around and avoid Kirilenko if possible. A powerful player can get easy dunks on this team.

WIZARDS

PLAYERS

NAME	NUMBER	SHOTS	DUNKS	BOARDS	POWER	BLOCKS	STEALS	HANDLES	QUICKS	GRAND TOTAL
ANTAWN JAMISON	4	75	90	70	75	40	21	55	70	503
LARRY HUGHES	20	70	85	55	40	30	65	70	80	515
GILBERT ARENAS	0	55	21	35	45	40	75	80	80	432
JUAN DIXON	3	75	25	25	21	11	60	80	85	385
KWAME BROWN	5	50	80	65	55	55	45	50	65	472

Antawn Jamison

This high-flying player can attack the rack with impunity. His shot ain't bad, either.

SUGGESTED LINEUP

- Larry Hughes (offense, steals)
- Antawn Jamison (offense)
- Gilbert Arenas (handles, steals)

Larry Hughes

Larry Hughes is known for scoring and dunking. But his good handles and defensive skills make him a truly complete player as well.

Gilbert Arenas

The one-time Warrior is a master of tricks and perimeter defense. Play up his strengths and he's an asset to the team.

BEING

Arenas and Hughes should handle the rock; Jamison and Hughes are your finishers. Do tricks with Arenas but pass up shots unless he's wide open.

On defense, you won't get far trying to block shots. You do have some talented thieves, though, so try to swipe the ball at every opportunity.

DEFEATING

Play off Jamison and Arenas, tempting them to shoot the rock. Stay closer on Hughes.

On the offensive end, pound the ball inside and jam it home. Let long-range shots fly if they leave you open; chances are, nobody's home to goaltend them.

Juan Dixon

Juan Dixon is another guy who's fast and masterful with the rock. He lacks the defensive skills of Arenas, but has a sweeter shot. Your personal playing style will determine who you like more.

Kwame Brown

The first high-school player ever selected No. 1 overall in the NBA draft, Kwame is still looking to make his mark on the league. His rim-rattling dunks are his most standout quality, though he plays good D as well.

LEGENDS

There are two types of Legends in *NBA STREET V3*: NBA Legends and Street Legends. We cover both flavors in this chapter.

NBA Legends

NBA Legends In-Game Stats									
NAME	NUMBER	SHOOTING	DUNKS	BOARDS	POWER	BLOCKS	STEALS	HANDLES	SPEED	GRAND TOTAL
JULIUS ERVING	32	75	99	50	55	41	61	75	85	573
CONNIE HAWKINS	42	60	85	75	60	70	55	50	70	569
EARL MONROE	15	75	21	50	45	40	65	90	80	481
ELGIN BAYLOR	22	70	81	65	80	30	45	55	80	530
BILL WALTON	32	50	80	90	70	61	41	40	65	531
EARVIN "MAGIC" JOHNSON	32	71	45	45	60	21	85	99	85	543
PETE MARAVICH	44	90	0	60	45	21	75	99	80	516
GEORGE GERVIN	44	80	70	45	35	41	70	75	70	533
DAVID THOMPSON	33	75	90	50	35	55	50	75	80	544
LARRY BIRD	33	99	10	55	70	25	75	81	55	503
CLYDE DREXLER	22	80	85	50	55	40	55	70	70	530
ISIAH THOMAS	11	75	10	30	45	21	85	90	99	466
DOMINIQUE WILKINS	21	70	99	60	60	40	50	55	80	536
MOSES MALONE	2	50	70	85	85	61	21	35	60	471
WILT CHAMBERLAIN	13	70	80	85	90	95	40	21	65	559
BILL RUSSELL	6	50	80	99	85	99	45	35	70	571
NATE ARCHIBALD	10	71	0	41	35	21	81	99	99	458
DARRYL DAWKINS	53	50	99	65	90	80	35	40	55	567
BOB COUSY	14	71	0	41	40	21	85	99	99	473
KAREEM ABDUL-JABBAR	33	85	75	90	70	90	50	50	50	593
SPUD WEBB	4	71	99	21	21	21	65	75	99	479
JOE DUMARS	4	75	0	35	35	35	90	99	85	461
WALT FRAZIER	10	81	0	35	35	21	99	85	85	453
RICK MAHORN	44	55	70	70	85	65	30	35	40	495
BERNARD KING	30	75	50	60	45	21	65	85	80	511

Julius Erving (Dr. J)

After a phenomenal collegiate career, the Julius Erving story had just begun. Erving was one of six players in NCAA history to average over 20 points and 20 rebounds a game. In 16 years with the ABA and NBA, the man known as "Dr. J" finished his pro career with four league MVP awards and an NBA championship in 1983. He is one of only three players in history to score more than 30,000 career points.

Height: 6'7" Weight: 200
College: Massachusetts
ABA Teams: Virginia (1971-72 to 1972-73), New York (1973-74 to 1975-76)
NBA Teams: Philadelphia 76ers (1976-87)

					NBA Totals						
G	FG%	3PFG%	FT%	REBS	RPG	ASTS	APG	STLS	BLKS	PTS	PPG
836	.507	.261	.777	5601	6.7	3224	3.9	1508	1293	18364	22.0

Connie Hawkins

One of the most creative players to ever play the game, Connie Hawkins was one of the first to bring the showy style of New York City playground street hoops to the pro game. Hawkins left the University of Iowa after his freshman year and started his career in the ABA, where he won the league MVP his rookie season. In 1970, Hawkins joined the NBA and played seven seasons with Phoenix, Los Angeles, and Atlanta.

Height: 6'8" Weight: 215
College: Iowa
ABA Teams: Pittsburgh (1967-68), Minnesota (1968-69)
NBA Teams: Phoenix (1969-73), Los Angeles (1973-75), Atlanta (1975)

				NBA Totals					
G	FG%	FT%	REBS	RPG	ASTS	APG		PTS	PPG
499	.467	.685	4432	6.1	917	1.3		8733	12.0

Earl Monroe

Once described as "the ultimate playground player," Earl Monroe slashed, spun, and cut his way into NBA stardom. An astounding ball handler who made off-balance shots and unthinkable baskets his forte, Earl "The Pearl" was a master of the one-on-one game. He was a four-time All-Star who finished with a career average of 18.8 points per game and a .464 career field-goal percentage in 13 seasons.

Height: 6'3" Weight: 190
College: Winston-Salem (N.C.)
NBA Teams: Baltimore (1967-71), New York (1971-80)

					NBA Totals						
G	FG%	FT%	REBS	RPG	ASTS	APG	STLS	BLKS	PTS	PPG
926	.464	.807	.2796	3.0	3594	3.9	473	121	17454	18.8

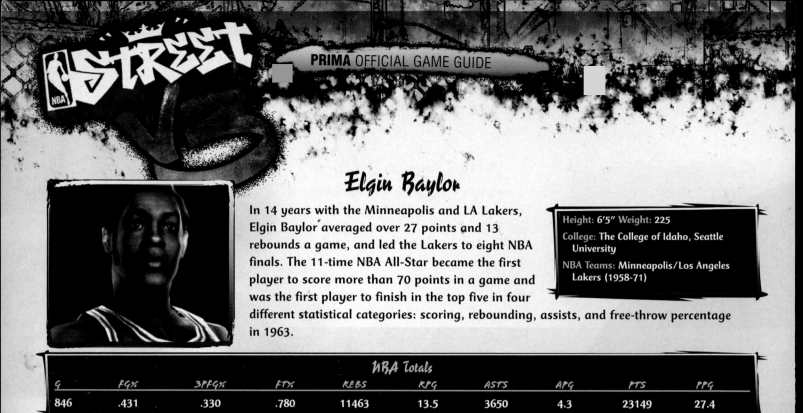

Elgin Baylor

In 14 years with the Minneapolis and LA Lakers, Elgin Baylor averaged over 27 points and 13 rebounds a game, and led the Lakers to eight NBA finals. The 11-time NBA All-Star became the first player to score more than 70 points in a game and was the first player to finish in the top five in four different statistical categories: scoring, rebounding, assists, and free-throw percentage in 1963.

Height: 6'5" Weight: 225
College: The College of Idaho, Seattle University
NBA Teams: Minneapolis/Los Angeles Lakers (1958-71)

NBA Totals

G	FGX	3PFGX	FTX	REBS	RPG	ASTS	APG	PTS	PPG
846	.431	.330	.780	11463	13.5	3650	4.3	23149	27.4

Bill Walton

Bill Walton was drafted #1 overall in 1974 by the NBA Portland Trail Blazers after leading UCLA to two national championships. He led Portland to its first NBA title in 1977. Traded by the LA Clippers to the Boston Celtics in 1985, the one-time league MVP won his second NBA title with the 1986 Celtics. Walton is one of four players to lead the league in both blocked shots and rebounding in the same season.

Height: 6'11" Weight: 235
College: UCLA
NBA Teams: Portland (1974-78), San Diego (1979-84), Los Angeles Clippers (1984-85), Boston (1985-87)

NBA Totals

G	FGX	FTX	REBS	RPG	ASTS	APG	STLS	BLKS	PTS	PPG
468	.521	.660	4923	10.5	1590	3.4	380	1034	6215	13.3

Earvin "Magic" Johnson

The fast-breaks, the no-look behind-the-back passes, the jump-hooks…Earvin Johnson was simply Magic. After capturing the national championship his senior season at Michigan State, Magic Johnson played 13 years for the LA Lakers. He won his first NBA championship in his second season and led LA to four more during the 1980s. The 12-time All-Star won the league's MVP award and Finals MVP award three times each.

Height: 6'9" Weight: 255
College: Michigan State
NBA Teams: Los Angeles Lakers (1979-91, 1996)

NBA Totals

G	FGX	3PFGX	FTX	REBS	RPG	ASTS	APG	STLS	BLKS	PTS	PPG
906	.520	.303	.848	6559	7.2	10141	11.2	1724	374	17707	19.5

Pete Maravich

With his amazing ballhandling skills and court vision, Pete Maravich brought the behind-the-back dribble and the through-the-legs pass to the mainstream of the NBA. His circus-like maneuvers and free-spirited style of play helped "Pistol Pete" earn five NBA All-Star berths. A true scorer, Maravich captured one league scoring title and was near the top of the assists category in all 10 of his NBA seasons.

Height: 6'5" Weight: 200
College: Louisiana State
NBA Teams: Atlanta (1970-74), New Orleans/Utah (1974-80), Boston (1980)

NBA Totals

G	FG%	3PFG%	FT%	REBS	RPG	ASTS	APG	STLS	BLKS	PTS	PPG
658	.441	.667	.820	2747	4.2	3563	5.4	587	108	15948	24.2

George "Ice Man" Gervin

George Gervin earned four NBA scoring titles in five seasons, third-best in league history, and finished with a career scoring average of 26.2 points per game. So consistent was Gervin, he had a streak of 407 consecutive games scoring in double figures, the fourth longest of all time. A nine-time NBA All-Star, Gervin led the Spurs to five division titles and finished second in voting for the league MVP two times.

Height: 6'7" Weight: 185
College: Long Beach St., Eastern Michigan
ABA Teams: Virginia (1972-73 to 1973-74), San Antonio (1973-74 to 1975-76)
NBA Teams: San Antonio (1976-85), Chicago (1985-86)

NBA Totals

G	FG%	3PFG%	FT%	REBS	RPG	ASTS	APG	STLS	BLKS	PTS	PPG
791	.511	.297	.844	3607	4.6	2214	2.8	941	670	20708	26.2

David Thompson

David Thompson was drafted in the first round by both pro leagues before signing with the ABA's Denver Nuggets in 1975. He earned Rookie of the Year and All-Star Game MVP. After the ABA and NBA merger, Thompson's triumphs continued with Denver, Seattle, and Indiana. He was named to four NBA All-Star teams, but his greatest moment came in 1978 when he scored 73 points in a single game, third-best in league history.

Height: 6'4" Weight: 195
College: North Carolina State
ABA Teams: Denver (1975-76)
NBA Teams: Denver (1976-82), Seattle (1982-84)

NBA Totals

G	FG%	3PFG%	FT%	REBS	RPG	ASTS	APG	STLS	BLKS	PTS	PPG
509	.504	.277	.778	1921	3.8	1631	3.2	459	407	11264	22.7

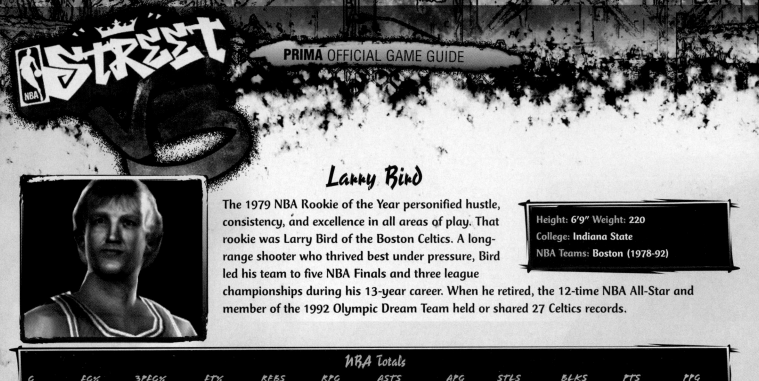

Larry Bird

The 1979 NBA Rookie of the Year personified hustle, consistency, and excellence in all areas of play. That rookie was Larry Bird of the Boston Celtics. A long-range shooter who thrived best under pressure, Bird led his team to five NBA Finals and three league championships during his 13-year career. When he retired, the 12-time NBA All-Star and member of the 1992 Olympic Dream Team held or shared 27 Celtics records.

Height: 6'9" Weight: 220
College: Indiana State
NBA Teams: Boston (1978-92)

NBA Totals

G	FG%	3PFG%	FT%	REBS	RPG	ASTS	APG	STLS	BLKS	PTS	PPG
897	.496	.376	.886	8974	10.0	5695	6.3	1556	755	21791	24.3

Clyde Drexler

The pro career of Clyde Drexler began in 1983 with the Portland Trail Blazers. Clyde "The Glide" led Portland to two Western Conference titles in three years only to fall short in the finals. In 1995, Drexler was traded to the Rockets and helped lead them to their second league title. When he retired, Drexler was one of three players in NBA history to finish with 20,000 points, 6,000 rebounds, and 3,000 assists.

Height: 6'7" Weight: 222
College: Houston
NBA Teams: Portland (1983-95), Houston (1995-98)

NBA Totals

G	FG%	3PFG%	FT%	REBS	RPG	ASTS	APG	BLKS	PTS	PPG
1086	.472	.318	.788	6677	6.1	6125	5.6	719	22195	20.4

Isiah Thomas

Isiah Thomas was one of the best small men to have played the game. A tenacious six-foot guard who played like a seven-footer, Thomas' determination and leadership skills turned an awful Detroit Piston team into a two-time NBA champion. During his astonishing career, Thomas was named to the All-Star team 12 times and was named NBA Finals MVP in 1990. He was the fourth player in league history to record 9,000 assists.

Height: 6'1" Weight: 182
College: Indiana
NBA Teams: Detroit Pistons (1981-94)

NBA Totals

G	FG%	3PFG%	FT%	REBS	RPG	ASTS	APG	STLS	BLKS	PTS	PPG
979	.452	.290	.759	3478	3.6	9061	9.3	1861	249	18822	19.2

Dominique Wilkins

One of only nine NBA players to score over 25,000 points, Dominique Wilkins averaged 20 or more points a game for 11 seasons in a row. In 1983 he made the NBA All-Rookie team, then went on to play on nine All-Star teams and captured the NBA's Slam-Dunk Championship during All-Star weekend twice. Wilkins' greatest achievement came in 1986 when he won the NBA scoring title with an average of 30.3 points per game.

Height: 6'8" Weight: 224
College: Georgia
NBA Teams: Atlanta (1982-94), Los Angeles Clippers (1994), Boston (1994-95), San Antonio (1996), Orlando (1999)

			NBA Totals								
G	FG%	3PFG%	FT%	REBS	RPG	ASTS	APG	STLS	BLKS	PTS	PPG
1074	.461	.811	.811	7169	6.7	2677	2.5	1378	642	26668	24.8

Moses Malone

Moses Malone turned pro straight out of high school and dominated the boards throughout his 21-year career. He started with the Utah Stars of the ABA and finished as the third-leading rebounder and fourth-leading scorer in pro history. Malone led his Houston Rockets to the 1981 NBA Finals and captured his first championship as a member of the 1983 Philadelphia 76ers.

Height: 6'10" Weight: 235
College: None
ABA Teams: Utah (1974-75 and 1975-76), St. Louis (1975-76)
NBA Teams: Buffalo Braves (1976-77), Houston (1977-82), Philadelphia (1982-86, 1993-94), Washington (1986-88), Atlanta (1988-91), Milwaukee (1991-93), San Antonio (1994-95)

			NBA Totals								
G	FG%	FT%	REBS	RPG	ASTS	APG	STLS	BLKS	PTS	PPG
1329	.491	.769	16212	12.2	1796	1.4	1089	1733	27409	20.6

Wilt Chamberlain

Wilt Chamberlain was a dominant force. Wilt "the Stilt" could score in almost any situation, at any time, against any player. His 100 points in one game stands as one of sports' seemingly unbreakable records. He also holds NBA single-game marks with 55 rebounds and 18 consecutive field goals. During the 1961-62 season, Chamberlain averaged an unbelievable 50.4 points per game. He was perhaps the greatest player ever.

Height: 7'1" Weight: 275
College: Kansas
NBA Teams: Philadelphia/Golden State (1959-65), Philadelphia (1965-68), Los Angeles Lakers (1968-73)

			NBA Totals						
G	FG%	FT%	REBS	RPG	ASTS	APG	PTS	PPG
1045	.540	.511	23924	22.9	4643	4.4	31419	30.1

Bill Russell

After two collegiate national championships at the University of San Francisco, Bill Russell led the NBA's Boston Celtics to 11 world titles in 13 seasons. Known for his defense, rebounding, and unselfish play, he earned the NBA's Most Valuable Player award five times and was named to 12 All-Star teams. Russell finished his career with 21,620 rebounds and averaged 22.5 points per game.

Height: 6'10" Weight: 220
College: San Francisco
NBA Teams: Boston (1956-77)

NBA Totals

G	FG%	FT%	REBS	RPG	ASTS	APG	PTS	PPG
963	.440	.561	21620	22.5	4100	4.3	14522	15.1

Nate Archibald

In 1972-73, Nate Archibald became the only NBA player to lead the league in scoring and assists in the same year. Averaging 34 points and 11.4 assists per game for that year, "Tiny" proved that he belonged with the big guys. Archibald finished his career ranked ninth on the all-time assists list. He was chosen for the All-Star Game six times and in 1996 was named one of the 50 greatest players of NBA history.

Height: 6'1" Weight: 160
College: Texas El-Paso
NBA Teams: Cincinnati/Kansas City (1970-76), New York Nets (1976-77), Buffalo (1977-78), Boston (1978-83), Milwaukee (1983-84)

NBA Totals

G	FG%	3PFG%	FT%	REBS	RPG	ASTS	APG	STLS	BLKS	PTS	PPG
876	.467	.224	.810	2046	2.3	6476	7.4	719	81	16481	18.8

Darryl Dawkins

One of the most flamboyant players in the game, Darryl Dawkins skipped college ball altogether and made the jump to the NBA from high school. Dawkins, who claimed to have come from the planet "Lovetron," was quick to make his mark on the league. Drafted #5 overall by the Philadelphia 76ers in 1975, he led his team to the NBA finals in only his third season. Dawkins is known for his dunk that shattered the backboard.

Height: 6'11" Weight: 252
College: None
NBA Teams: Philadelphia (1975-82), New Jersey (1982-87), Utah (1987-88), Detroit (1988-89)

NBA Totals

G	FG%	FT%	REBS	RPG	ASTS	APG	PTS	PPG
726	.572	.685	4432	6.1	917	1.3	8733	12.0

Bob Cousy

Nicknamed "The Houdini of the Hardwood," Boston's Bob Cousy was one of the first players to bring flair and pizzazz to the game. "The Cooz," who led the league in assists eight consecutive seasons, helped lead the Boston Celtics to six NBA titles and was named to 13 All-Star teams. A career 80 percent free throw shooter, Cousy finished his career averaging 7.5 assists and 18.4 points per game.

Height: 6'7" **Weight:** 185
College: Holy Cross
NBA Teams: Boston (1950-63), Cincinnati Royals (1969-70)

NBA Totals

G	FG%	3PFG%	FT%	REBS	RPG	ASTS	APG	PTS	PPG
924	0.375	0.376	0.803	4,786	5.2	6,955	7.5	16,960	18.4

Kareem Abdul-Jabbar

When Kareem Abdul-Jabbar left the game in 1989 at age 42, no NBA player had ever scored more points, blocked more shots, won more Most Valuable Player awards, played in more All-Star Games or logged more seasons. His list of personal and team accomplishments is perhaps the most awesome in league history: Rookie of the Year, member of 6 NBA championship teams, 6-time NBA MVP, 2-time NBA Finals MVP, 19-time All-Star, 2-time scoring champion, and a member of the NBA 35th and 50th Anniversary All-Time Teams. He also owned eight playoff records and seven All-Star records. No player achieved as much individual and team success as did Abdul-Jabbar.

Height: 7'2" **Weight:** 267
College: None
NBA Teams: Milwaukee (1969-75), Los Angeles Lakers (1975-89)

NBA Totals

G	FG%	3PFG%	FT%	REBS	RPG	ASTS	APG	STLS	BLKS	PTS	PPG
1,560	0.559	0.056	0.721	17,440	11.2	5,660	3.6	1,160	3,189	38,387	24.6

Spud Webb

One of the most remarkable physical talents ever to play in the NBA, the 5-foot, 7-inch Webb played 12 seasons but is perhaps best remembered for the 1986 Slam Dunk contest. Despite his diminutive size, he won that contest, beating out some of the most electrifying dunkers in the league—including his teammate Dominique Wilkins, the "Human Highlight Film."

Height: 5'7" **Weight:** 133
College: North Carolina State
NBA Teams: Atlanta (1985-91; 1995-96), Sacramento (1991-95), Minnesota (1995-96), Orlando (1997-98)

NBA Totals

G	FG%	3PFG%	FT%	REBS	RPG	ASTS	APG	STLS	BLKS	PTS	PPG
814	.452	.314	.848	1742	2.1	4342	5.33	922	111	8072	9.9

Joe Dumars

An integral part of Detroit's "Bad Boy" teams of the late '80s and early '90s, the quiet Joe Dumars seemed incongruous on teams filled with big, aggressive personalities. But he let his play do the talking, and he quickly earned a reputation as a deadly shooter and tenacious defender. It's a testament to his outstanding character that, despite the rough-and-tumble mystique of those Pistons teams, the NBA's sportsmanship award is now named the Joe Dumars Trophy.

Height: 6'3" Weight: 195
College: McNeese State
NBA Teams: Detroit (1985-99)

NBA Totals

G	FG%	3PFG%	FT%	REBS	RPG	ASTS	APG	STLS	BLKS	PTS	PPG
1018	.460	.382	.843	2,203	2.20	4,612	4.5	902	83	16401	16.1

Walt Frazier

Walt Frazier and New York City. It was a match made in heaven. The man known to most as "Clyde" electrified New York Knick fans for 10 seasons with a blend of smooth drives, mid-range jump shots, and a stingy defensive style of play. The 1967 Rookie of the Year led the Knicks to the 1970 and 1973 NBA titles. "Clyde" finished his career with seven All-Star selections and seven NBA's All-Defensive First Team awards.

Height: 6'4" Weight: 200
College: Southern Illinois University
NBA Teams: New York (1967-77),
Cleveland (1977-80)

NBA Totals

G	FG%	FT%	REBS	RPG	ASTS	APG	PTS	PPG
825	.490	.786	4830	5.9	5040	6.1	15581	18.9

Rick Mahorn

Rick Mahorn was member of the famed "Bad Boys" Detroit teams, and won an NBA Championship with them in 1989. Slightly undersized for the center position, he more than made up for it with his overpowering, physical brand of play. He later was traded to the Philadelphia 76ers, where he became half of a formidable tandem with Charles Barkley.

Height: 6'10" Weight: 260
College: Hampton Institute
NBA Teams: Washington (1980-84),
Detroit (1985-88; 1996,97), Philadelphia
(1989-90), New Jersey (1992-95)

NBA Totals

G	FG%	3PFG%	FT%	REBS	RPG	ASTS	APG	STLS	BLKS	PTS	PPG
1,117	.493	.132	.704	6,957	6.20	1,082	1.0	633	1,007	7,763	6.9

Bernard King

One of the most explosive scorers of his era, Bernard King had a fascinating career. Major knee reconstruction cost him two years at the peak of his abilities. When he returned to the court despite great odds against a comeback, he had to adjust his style of play to accommodate his diminished physical abilities. He proved many skeptics wrong when he became an All-Star. He poured in more than 19,000 points in a career spent with the New Jersey Nets, Utah Jazz, Golden State Warriors, New York Knicks, and Washington Bullets.

Height: 6'7" Weight: 205
College: **Tennessee**
NBA Teams: **New Jersey (1977-79; 1992-93), Utah (1979-80), Golden State (1980-82), New York (1982-87), Washington (1987-91)**

NBA Totals

G	FG%	3PFG%	FT%	REBS	RPG	ASTS	APG	STLS	BLKS	PTS	PPG
874	0.518	0.172	0.73	5,060	5.8	2,863	3.3	866	230	19,655	22.5

Street Legends

Street Legends Stats

NAME	SHOOTING	DUNKS	BOARDS	POWER	BLOCKS	STEALS	HANDLES	SPEED	GRAND TOTAL
BIGGIE LITTLES	80	0	60	40	30	90	99	99	498
DIME	80	61	40	40	60	99	90	80	552
TAKASHI	51	80	85	75	99	41	10	55	497
PHAT	70	70	99	99	75	40	35	40	531
BONAFIDE	70	90	99	80	60	80	80	99	658
STRETCH	80	95	80	40	80	60	60	50	548

Biggie Littles

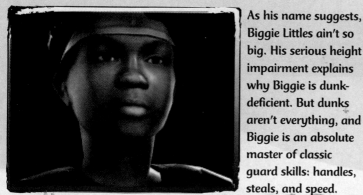

As his name suggests, Biggie Littles ain't so big. His serious height impairment explains why Biggie is dunk-deficient. But dunks aren't everything, and Biggie is an absolute master of classic guard skills: handles, steals, and speed.

He's also a sweet shooter, and his ability to board is surprising considering his size.

Dime

Another fast, top-notch ball handler, Dime is a steal specialist. Nobody is more proficient at thieving the ball—*nobody*. Dime's shot is sweet, too.

Stretch

Stretch is tall and lean. As you might expect, that means he can execute great blocks and exceptional dunks—though he's a little light on power, so he can get rocked by burly opponents. Fortunately for him, he's also got a silky-smooth shot, so he can torment the tough guys if they're muscling him out of the lane.

Takashi

A practitioner of classic center skills, Takashi is one of the top shot-blockers in the game. He can also board and dunk with the best of them, and he brings a lot of power to the court.

Phat

Phat's nickname says it all. He's not exactly fast or skilled at tricks. But he's a true monster on the boards, and nobody's stronger. Pair this up with his great dunk skill, and you've got a player who won't be denied in the lane. Add to this his excellent shot-blocking, and you have a true monster in the paint.

Bonafide

Bonafide is the real deal; he can do it all. Dunks and boards are his tip-top abilities, but make no mistake: he can shoot, steal, block shots, you name it. You'd be hard-pressed to find a more complete player, anywhere.

UNLOCKABLES

Many of the Legends, courts, banners, and clothes in *NBA STREET V3* are locked when you first start to play. You can unlock most of this stuff in two ways. First, you can buy it with Street Points. Second, you can unlock specific players, items, and locations by winning specific challenges.

It's tempting to spend Street Points to unlock cool stuff right away, but we recommend holding off. Unlock as much as possible by winning challenges and then use Street Points to buy anything that's left over.

Player Unlocks

Unlockable Street Legends

PLAYER	STATUS AT START	WHERE UNLOCKED	STREET POINT VALUE
BEASTIE BOYS (TEAM)	Locked	Street Challenge: Win the 5 Boroughs Tournament	500
BIGGIE LITTLES	Locked	Street Challenge: Win the Biggie Littles Is Back or Doing Big Things Tournament	1000
DIME	Locked	Street Challenge: Win the Can You Spare a Dime or Dropped by Dime Tournament	1500
TAKASHI	Locked	Street Challenge: Win the Takashi Returns or Hand of the Rising Sun Tournament	2000
PHAT	Locked	Street Challenge: Win the Big Kid on the Block or Texas Sized Game Tournament	2500
BONAFIDE	Locked	Street Challenge: Win the Certified Bonafide or Undisputed Tournament	3000
STRETCH	Locked	Street Challenge: Win the Respect Your Elders or Still Reigning Tournament	4000

Unlockable NBA Legends

PLAYER	STATUS AT START	WHERE UNLOCKED	STREET POINT VALUE
RICK MAHORN	Unlocked	—	—
JOE DUMARS	Unlocked	—	—
DARRYL DAWKINS	Unlocked	—	—
SPUD WEBB	Unlocked	—	—
CONNIE HAWKINS	Locked	Street Challenge: Win an Old School Legend Event	500
DAVID THOMPSON	Locked	Street Challenge: Win the Dunks Only With DT Event	500
BOB COUSEY	Locked	Street Challenge: Win an Old School Legend Event	500

Unlockable NBA Legends (cont'd)

PLAYER	STATUS AT START	WHERE UNLOCKED	STREET POINT VALUE
EARL MONROE	Locked	Street Challenge: Win the Earl the Pearl Is Back Event	1000
ELGIN BAYLOR	Locked	Street Challenge: Win an Old School Legend Event	1000
CLYDE DREXLER	Locked	Street Challenge: Win the Dunks Only With the Glide Event	1000
WALT FRAZIER	Locked	Street Challenge: Win an Old School Legend Event	1000
NATE ARCHIBALD	Locked	Street Challenge: Win an Old School Legend Event	1500
BERNARD KING	Locked	Street Challenge: Win the Long Live the King Event	2000
BILL WALTON	Locked	Street Challenge: Win an Old School Legend Event	2000
GEORGE GERVIN	Locked	Street Challenge: Win an Old School Legend Event	2000
MOSES MALONE	Locked	Street Challenge: Win the Moses Malone Is Back Event	2000
ISIAH THOMAS	Locked	Street Challenge: Win the Zeke Is Getting Tricky Event	2500
DOMINIQUE WILKINS	Locked	Street Challenge: Win the Human Highlight Film Event	2500
PETE MARAVICH	Locked	Street Challenge: Win an Old School Legend Event	3000
BILL RUSSELL	Locked	Street Challenge: Win an Old School Legend Event	3000
JULIUS ERVING	Locked	Street Challenge: Win the Doctor Is In Event	4000
MAGIC JOHNSON	Locked	Street Challenge: Win the Magic Show Event	4000
LARRY BIRD	Locked	Street Challenge: Win the Larry Legend Event	4000
WILT CHAMBERLAIN	Locked	Street Challenge: Win an Old School Legend Event	4000
KAREEM ABDUL-JABBAR	Locked	Street Challenge: Win the Kareem Is Back Event	4000

Court Unlocks

Unlockable Courts

COURT	STATUS AT START	WHERE UNLOCKED	STREET POINT VALUE
THE HAWK	Unlocked	—	—
THE CAGE	Unlocked	—	—
FOSS PARK	Unlocked	—	—
TANDY	Unlocked	—	—
THE DOME	Locked	Street Challenge: Reach and maintain a Rep of 125	250
MACGREGOR PARK	Locked	Street Challenge: Reach and maintain a Rep of 150	500
BRIGHTON BEACH	Locked	Street Challenge: Reach and maintain a Rep of 200	750
VENICE BEACH (DAY)	Locked	Street Challenge: Reach and maintain a Rep of 250	1000
GUN HILL (DAY)	Locked	Street Challenge: Reach and maintain a Rep of 300	1250
VENICE BEACH (NIGHT)	Locked	Street Challenge: Reach and maintain a Rep of 350	1500
DYCKMAN (DAY)	Locked	Street Challenge: Reach and maintain a Rep of 400	1750
GUN HILL (NIGHT)	Locked	Street Challenge: Reach and maintain a Rep of 450	2000
MOSSWOOD (DAY)	Locked	Street Challenge: Reach and maintain a Rep of 500	2250
DYCKMAN (NIGHT)	Locked	Street Challenge: Reach and maintain a Rep of 550	2500
RUCKER PARK (DAY)	Locked	Street Challenge: Reach and maintain a Rep of 600	2750
MOSSWOOD (NIGHT)	Locked	Street Challenge: Reach and maintain a Rep of 650	3000
RUCKER PARK (NIGHT)	Locked	Street Challenge: Reach and maintain a Rep of 700	4000

Court Banner Unlocks

Unlockable Banners

BANNER	STATUS AT START	WHERE UNLOCKED	STREET POINT VALUE
STREET V3 ORANGE	Locked	Street Challenge: Win the Last Chance at Glory Tournament	250
STREET V3 GOLD	Locked	Street Challenge: Win the Big Finish or the Grand Finale Tournament	250

Unlockable Banners (cont'd)

BANNER	STATUS AT START	WHERE UNLOCKED	STREET POINT VALUE
CONCRETE WHITE	Locked	Street Challenge: Win the EA SPORTS BIG™ Concrete Classic Tournament at The Hawk	500
CONCRETE LIGHT BLUE	Locked	Street Challenge: Win the EA SPORTS BIG™ Concrete Classic Tournament at Gun Hill	500
CONCRETE BLUE	Locked	Street Challenge: Win the EA SPORTS BIG™ Concrete Classic Tournament at Brighton Beach	500
ROUNDBALL 1	Locked	Street Challenge: Win an EA SPORTS™ Roundball Classic Tournament at Foss Park	500
ROUNDBALL 2	Locked	Street Challenge: Win an EA SPORTS™ Roundball Classic Tournament at Foss Park	500
THE CAGE GREEN	Locked	Street Challenge: Win the Biggie Littles Is Back Tournament	500
THE CAGE BLACK	Locked	Street Challenge: Win the Doing Big Things Tournament	500
THE DOME GOLD	Locked	Street Challenge: Win the Can You Spare a Dime Tournament	500
THE DOME WHITE	Locked	Street Challenge: Win the Dropped by Dime Tournament	500
VENICE WHITE	Locked	Street Challenge: Win the Takashi Returns Tournament	500
VENICE LIGHT BLUE	Locked	Street Challenge: Win the Hand of the Rising Sun Tournament	500
MACGREGOR 1	Locked	Street Challenge: Win the Big Kid on the Block Tournament	500
MACGREGOR 2	Locked	Street Challenge: Win the Texas Sized Game Tournament	500
DYCKMAN BLUE	Locked	Street Challenge: Win the Certified Bonafide Tournament	500
DYCKMAN LIGHT BLUE	Locked	Street Challenge: Win the Undisputed Tournament	500
RUCKER GREEN	Locked	Street Challenge: Win the Respect Your Elders Tournament	500
RUCKER RED	Locked	Street Challenge: Win the Still Reigning Tournament	500
V3-ON-3 DYCKMAN	Locked	Street Challenge: Win the Street V3-On-3 Tournament at Dyckman	500
RBK VENICE	Locked	Street Challenge: Win the Rbk Invitational Tournament at Venice Beach	1000
RBK RUCKER	Locked	Street Challenge: Win the Rbk Invitational Tournament at Rucker Park	1000
CITY NAME BLACK	Locked	Street Challenge: Win a Streetball Royalty Tournament	1000
CITY NAME GOLD	Locked	Street Challenge: Win a Streetball Royalty Tournament	1000

LEGENDS

Hat Unlocks

Unlockable Hats

HAT	STATUS AT START	WHERE UNLOCKED	STREET POINT VALUE
RBK CHARLOTTE BOBCATS	Locked	Street Challenge: Win the Dunks Only With Gerald Wallace Event	50
RBK CHICAGO BULLS	Locked	Street Challenge: Win the Kirk Hinrich Is Getting Tricky Event	50
RBK PORTLAND TRAIL BLAZERS	Locked	Street Challenge: Win the Damon Stoudamire Is Getting Tricky Event	50
RBK TORONTO RAPTORS	Locked	Street Challenge: Win the Skip to My Lou Is Getting Tricky Event	50
RBK MEMPHIS GRIZZLIES	Locked	Street Challenge: Win the Jason Williams Is Getting Tricky Event	50
RBK LA CLIPPERS	Locked	Street Challenge: Win the Dunks Only With Corey Maggette Event	50
RBK ATLANTA HAWKS	Locked	Street Challenge: Win the Antoine Walker Event	50
RBK WASHINGTON WIZARDS	Locked	Street Challenge: Win the Dunks Only With Antawn Jamison Event	50
RBK DETROIT PISTONS	Locked	Street Challenge: Win the Richard Hamilton Event	50
RBK DENVER NUGGETS	Locked	Street Challenge: Win the Carmelo Anthony Event	50
RBK UTAH JAZZ	Locked	Street Challenge: Win the Andrei Kirilenko Event	50
RBK SACRAMENTO KINGS	Locked	Street Challenge: Win the Mike Bibby Is Getting Tricky Event	50
RBK SEATTLE SONICS	Locked	Street Challenge: Win the Ray Allen Event	50
RBK PHOENIX SUNS	Locked	Street Challenge: Win the Dunks Only With Amare Event	50
RBK MIAMI HEAT	Locked	Street Challenge: Win the Dwyane Wade Event	50
RBK BOSTON CELTICS	Locked	Street Challenge: Win the Paul Pierce Event	50
RBK DALLAS MAVERICKS	Locked	Street Challenge: Win the Dirk Nowitzki Event	50
RBK INDIANA PACERS	Locked	Street Challenge: Win the Jermaine O'Neal Event	50
RBK NEW YORK KNICKS	Locked	Street Challenge: Win the Starbury Is Getting Tricky Event	50
RBK PHILADELPHIA 76ERS	Locked	Street Challenge: Win the Allen Iverson Event	50
RBK MINNESOTA TIMBERWOLVES	Locked	Street Challenge: Win the Kevin Garnett Event	50

Unlockable Hats (cont'd)

HAT	STATUS AT START	WHERE UNLOCKED	STREET POINT VALUE
RBK SAN ANTONIO SPURS	Locked	Street Challenge: Win the Tim Duncan Event	50
RBK NEW ORLEANS HORNETS	Locked	Street Challenge: Defeat Baron Davis in a Head 2 Head Dunk Contest	50
RBK MILWAUKEE BUCKS	Locked	Street Challenge: Defeat Desmond Mason in a Head 2 Head Dunk Contest	50
RBK ORLANDO MAGIC	Locked	Street Challenge: Defeat Steve Francis in a Head 2 Head Dunk Contest	50
RBK GOLDEN STATE WARRIORS	Locked	Street Challenge: Defeat Jason Richardson in a Head 2 Head Dunk Contest	50
RBK HOUSTON ROCKETS	Locked	Street Challenge: Defeat Tracy McGrady in a Head 2 Head Dunk Contest	50
RBK LA LAKERS	Locked	Street Challenge: Defeat Kobe Bryant in a Head 2 Head Dunk Contest	50
RBK NEW JERSEY NETS	Locked	Street Challenge: Defeat Vince Carter in a Head 2 Head Dunk Contest	50

Jersey Unlocks

NOTE: Certain jerseys can only be purchased with Street Points: there's no other way to unlock them.

EA Jerseys

JERSEY	STATUS AT START	WHERE UNLOCKED	STREET POINT VALUE
EA SPORTS™ ROUNDBALL CLASSIC 1	Locked	Street Challenge: Win an EA SPORTS™ Roundball Classic Tournament at Foss Park	150
EA SPORTS™ ROUNDBALL CLASSIC 2	Locked	Street Challenge: Win an EA SPORTS™ Roundball Classic Tournament at Foss Park	150
EA SPORTS™ ROUNDBALL CLASSIC WARMUP 1	Locked	Street Challenge: Win the EA SPORTS™ Roundball Classic Tournament at Mosswood Park	250

Old School Jerseys (Home and Away)

JERSEY	STATUS AT START	WHERE UNLOCKED	STREET POINT VALUE
85-86 BOSTON CELTICS	Locked	—	350
61-62 LOS ANGELES LAKERS	Locked	—	350
75-76 NEW YORK NETS	Locked	—	350

Old School Jerseys (Home and Away) (cont'd)

JERSEY	STATUS AT START	WHERE UNLOCKED	STREET POINT VALUE
66-67 PHILADELPHIA 76ERS	Locked	—	350
67-68 PITTSBURGH PIPERS	Locked	—	350
82-83 PHILADELPHIA 76ERS	Locked	—	350
91-92 PORTLAND TRAIL BLAZERS	Locked	—	350
79-80 SAN ANTONIO SPURS	Locked	—	350

Hardwood Classics Jerseys

JERSEY	STATUS AT START	WHERE UNLOCKED	STREET POINT VALUE
71-72 ATLANTA HAWKS—AWAY	Locked	—	500
77-78 WASHINGTON BULLETS—HOME	Locked	—	500
83-84 CHICAGO BULLS—AWAY	Locked	—	500
87-88 DENVER NUGGETS—AWAY	Locked	—	500
94-95 HOUSTON ROCKETS—AWAY	Locked	—	500
49-50 MINNEAPOLIS LAKERS—AWAY	Locked	—	500
64-65 PHILADELPHIA 76ERS—HOME	Locked	—	500
79-80 SAN ANTONIO SPURS—AWAY	Locked	—	500
82-83 PHILADELPHIA 76ERS—AWAY	Locked	—	500
75-76 NEW YORK NETS—AWAY	Locked	—	500
72-73 NEW YORK KNICKS—AWAY	Locked	—	500
76-77 NEW ORLEANS JAZZ—AWAY	Locked	—	500
79-80 LOS ANGELES LAKERS—AWAY	Locked	—	500
61-62 LOS ANGELES LAKERS—AWAY	Locked	—	500
88-89 DETROIT PISTONS—AWAY	Locked	—	500
85-86 BOSTON CELTICS—AWAY	Locked	—	500
79-80 ATLANTA HAWKS—AWAY	Locked	—	500
RBK 87-88 SACRAMENTO KINGS—AWAY	Locked	—	500
RBK 70-71 PORTLAND TRAIL BLAZERS—HOME	Locked	—	500
RBK 93-94 ORLANDO MAGIC—AWAY	Locked	—	500
RBK 79-80 NEW YORK KNICKS—HOME	Locked	—	500
RBK 54-55 SYRACUSE NATIONALS—AWAY	Locked	—	500
RBK 59-60 MINNEAPOLIS LAKERS—AWAY	Locked	—	500
RBK 87-88 INDIANA PACERS—AWAY	Locked	—	500
RBK 71-72 HOUSTON ROCKETS—AWAY	Locked	—	500
RBK 66-67 SAN FRANCISCO WARRIORS—AWAY	Locked	—	500
RBK 80-81 DETROIT PISTONS—HOME	Locked	—	500
RBK 75-76 DENVER NUGGETS—AWAY	Locked	—	500
RBK 83-84 DALLAS MAVERICKS—AWAY	Locked	—	500
RBK 75-76 CLEVELAND CAVALIERS—HOME	Locked	—	500
RBK 70-71 WASHINGTON BULLETS—AWAY	Locked	—	500

Shoe Unlocks

Unlockable Shoes

SHOES	STATUS AT START	WHERE UNLOCKED	STREET POINT VALUE
RBK ATR BOOM DIZZLE—WHITE/SILVER	Locked	Street Challenge: Win the Rbk 3-on-3 Challenge 1 Event	500
RBK S CARTER BB 11—WHITE/BLUE	Locked	Street Challenge: Win the Rbk 3-on-3 Challenge 2 Event	500
RBK CL BB FISSURE—BROWN	Locked	Street Challenge: Win the Rbk 3-on-3 Challenge 3 Event	500
RBK BOULEVARD	Locked	Street Challenge: Win the EA SPORTS BIG™ Concrete Classic Tournament at Brighton Beach	500
RBK BLACKTOP PUMP	Locked	Street Challenge: Win the EA SPORTS BIG™ Concrete Classic Tournament at Gun Hill	500
RBK QUESTION 11 MID—BLACK/BLACK	Locked	Street Challenge: Win an Rbk Invitational Tournament at Rucker Park	500
RBK ATR PUMP—WHITE/BLUE/RED	Locked	Street Challenge: Win the Rbk Challenge Dunk Contest Tournament	1000
RBK ATR CLEAR OUT	Locked	Street Challenge: Win the Rbk Invitational Tournament at Venice Beach	1500
RBK HIGH POST—BLACK/RED	Locked	Street Challenge: Win an Rbk Invitational Tournament at Rucker Park	1500
RBK HIGH POST—WHITE/RED	Locked	Street Challenge: Win the History Lesson Part 1 Dunk Contest Tournament	1500
RBK ATR 2ND COMING—WHITE/BLUE	Locked	Street Challenge: Win the History Lesson Part 2 Dunk Contest Tournament	1500
RBK ANSWER 8—WHITE/RED	Locked	Street Challenge: Win the Future Of Flight Dunk Contest Tournament	1500
RBK ANSWER 8—WHITE/BLACK	Locked	Street Challenge: Win the Legendary Status Dunk Contest Tournament	1500

Trophies

Unlockable Trophies

TROPHY	STATUS AT START	WHERE UNLOCKED	STREET POINT VALUE
FUTURE OF FLIGHT	Locked	Street Challenge: Win the Future of Flight Dunk Contest Tournament	—
RBK CHALLENGE	Locked	Street Challenge: Win the Rbk Challenge Dunk Contest Tournament	—
NEW YORK	Locked	Street Challenge: Win the New York Dunk Contest Tournament	—
LEGENDARY STATUS	Locked	Street Challenge: Win the Legendary Status Dunk Contest Tournament	—
HISTORY LESSON PART 1	Locked	Street Challenge: Win the History Lesson Part 1 Dunk Contest Tournament	—
HISTORY LESSON PART 2	Locked	Street Challenge: Win the History Lesson Part 2 Dunk Contest Tournament	—

Note - **The only unlockable rewards that can't be purchased with Street Points are Dunk Contest trophies. You must win Dunk Contests to get your hands on those.**

Now Available

NFL STREET 2
PRIMA OFFICIAL GAME GUIDE

INSIDE YOU'LL FIND:

Rosters and playbooks for all NFL and unlockable teams

Proven tactics for building a knock-out team

Tips for all gameplay modes, from the NFL Challenge to online play

Full field coverage

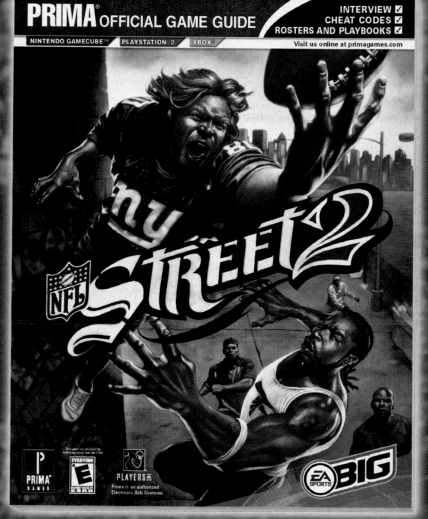

PRIMA® OFFICIAL GAME GUIDE

NINTENDO GAMECUBE™ PLAYSTATION 2 XBOX

INTERVIEW ☑
CHEAT CODES ☑
ROSTERS AND PLAYBOOKS ☑

Visit us online at primagames.com

NFL STREET 2

EA SPORTS BIG

EVERYONE
E
CONTENT RATED BY ESRB

Prima is an authorized Electronic Arts licensee.

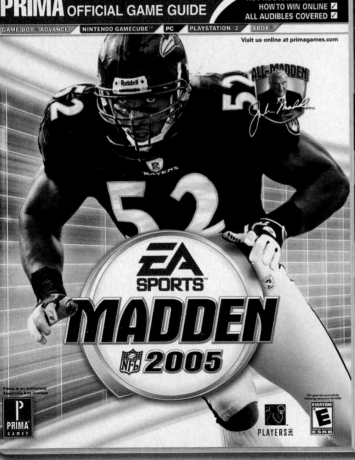